MW00773613

Jesus Trail

and Jerusalem

Jacob Saar

Author of the Israel National Trail guide

Eshkol Publishing Ltd. Israel

Language Editor: Shulamit Berman

Photography: Jacob Saar

Printed in Israel

Any information included in this guide might not be entirely accurate and up to date and the possibility of an error can never be eliminated. The publishers can accept no responsibility for inaccuracies and omissions. Your comments however, are always appreciated. Please send your comments to:

jesustrailhike@gmail.com

 Copyright for maps in this guide:

For most recent trail updates please visit:

http://jesustrail.com

ISBN 978-965-91249-5-4

Table of Contents

Front cover

Left: The Church of the Beatitudes.

Middle: Sea of Galilee as viewed from above the Church of the Primacy of St. Peter.

Right: Mt. Tabor as viewed from Mt. Precipice.

Back cover: Gethsemane – The Church of all Nations.

Hiking the Jesus Trail

Many holy places in the world are visited by millions of people who make pilgrimages in order to draw closer to God. But there is really only one Holy Land and that is the Land of Israel, where God showed the world how to live in peace according to his commandments. *The great poet Goethe said: "Who wishes to understand the poet must go to the poet's land."* Similarly, hiking the land of Jesus is a way of understanding the Lord.

The Jesus Trail, an initiative of Maoz Inon from Nazareth and his American partner Dave Landis, provides pilgrims with the only real opportunity to follow in the footsteps of Jesus. Marking of the trail was completed in honor of the visit of Pope Benedict XVI to the Holy land in May 2009. You will visit the Basilica of the Annunciation and Mount Precipice in Nazareth. Pope Benedict XVI delivered a mass on Mount Precipice during his visit to the Holy Land in the presence of more than 40,000 believers.

From Nazareth the trail continues to Zippori, the magnificent city built by Herod Antipas. In Cana the trail passes the wedding church where Jesus turned water into wine. John 2:11: *"This, the first of his miraculous signs, Jesus performed at Cana in Galilee. He thus revealed his glory, and his disciples put their faith in him."*

After hiking on an ancient Roman road you will arrive at the Horns of Hattin, site of the famous Battle of Hattin, which was fought in 1187 between the Crusader Kingdom of Jerusalem and Saladin. Descending from the Horns of Hattin you will pass the tomb of Nabi Shu'ayb - the biblical prophet Jethro –a central figure in the Druze religion. From Mount Arbel you will enjoy a magnificent view of the Sea of Galilee, Tabgha, the Mount of Beatitudes and Capernaum. In Tabgha the trail leads to the Church of the Multiplication, situated at site where Jesus fed more than 5000 people with five loaves of bread and two fish. *Matthew 14:19, 21: "And he directed the people to sit down on the grass. Taking the five loaves and the two fish and looking up to heaven, he gave thanks and broke the loaves. The number of those who ate was about five thousand men, besides women and children."*

Overlooking Tabgha, the Mount of Beatitudes where Jesus delivered the Sermon of the Mount is your next stop on the Jesus Trail. Here more than 200,000 believers attended Pope John Paul II's mass during his visit to the Holy Land in 2000. Your next destination is the splendid Domus Galilaeae, built on a hill just above the Mount of Beatitudes. The hike along the Sea of Galilee passes the Church of the Primacy of St. Peter and continues on to Capernaum, home of St. Peter and the site where the first four disciples, James, John, Peter and Andrew were chosen. On the south side of the Sea of Galilee you will come to the Yardenit baptism site on the River Jordan. A day and a half later you will climb Mount Tabor, believed to be the site of the Transfiguration. *Luke 9:30: "Two men, Moses and Elijah, appeared in glorious splendor, talking with Jesus."* The visit of Pope Paul VI to the Holy Land in January 1964 is commemorated on Mt. Tabor. From Mount Tabor the trail arrives back at Nazareth.

No hike of the Jesus Trail is complete without a visit to Jerusalem. You can hike the Israel National Trail from Nazareth to Jerusalem, or take a bus and complete the pilgrimage in Jerusalem. The final stage of the pilgrimage starts in the Judean Mountains at Ein Hindak. After a short hike you will pass the entrance to the Church of the Visitation in Ein Karem, which is built over the site where St. John the Baptist's parents lived. After another hour you will enter Jerusalem. From the Hebron road it is only10 kilometers to Bethlehem and the Church of the Nativity. At the southwest corner of the Old City of Jerusalem the trail passes just minutes from the Room of the Last Supper. From there you will continue to Mt. Olives and Gethsemane. Before entering the Old City you will visit Mary's Tomb. The trail ends at the Via Dolorosa and the Holy Sepulchre.

Each year millions of people visit the Holy Places. You will be among those who have truly followed in the footsteps of Jesus.

Preface

Please read the entire guide and study the maps before you start planning your trip.

Hike description

The header of each day contains: The starting point, the end point and the length in kilometers (1.6 km = 1 mi). The length is rounded up to the next kilometer. The second line includes the relevant map number(s), how much water to carry, and places to refill along the route. The hiking profile includes the height in meters above sea level, length of the day in kilometers, and few way points along the day. The hike description is printed in a regular font, starting each day at (0.0, meters). Numbers in parentheses indicate the distance in kilometers from the beginning of the day, and the height in meters above or (–) below sea level of the way point.

Water

In the northern part of the country you should fill about 3-4 liters of water in the morning and refill during the day as necessary. Water is available in villages, kibbutzim, towns, gas stations and other places along the trail. If you plan on hiking longer distances than recommended here, you will require more water. On hot days you should carry more water, up to 5 liters a day. The amount of drinking water recommended for each day's hike is included at the beginning of the daily hike description. Weather conditions and temperatures below 30°C have been taken into consideration for calculating how much water you will need. The recommended length of the hike and the landscape (ascents, flat land, etc.) and a load not exceeding 15 kg/person including water and food, are also factors that determine the amount of water to carry. **Caution**: Water used for agricultural purposes cannot be used for drinking.

When to hike?

Spring is the best time of year for the trek. The weather is mild at this time of the year and the spring blossoms are splendid. Winters in Israel are relatively mild. However, in winter you will experience more delays due to poor weather. Fall, from September to early December, is also a good season for hiking. Although the summer is hot and is the least recommended season, you can start hiking very early in the morning, at sunrise or even earlier. At about 10:00 find some shade, rest until 15:00-16:00 when the temperatures drop, and then you can continue the hike until sunset. Keep informed about weather conditions and adapt your schedule accordingly.

Get in shape

Start your preparations before you plan to arrive in Israel. Put on your new hiking shoes and hit the trails and sidewalks in your neighborhood. After a few weeks, when blisters are no longer a hazard, fill your backpack with a load of at least 10 kilos, and continue with your daily walking routine. My preparations included a 7-km walk in 1 hour without the backpack. I did this for 2-3 weeks, 4 times a week. In addition, I made two weekend trips of 15 kilometers with my fully loaded backpack, and it did the job for me. There are many other ways to prepare yourself physically, both in the gym and outside.

Hike and rest

It is recommended that you take a short break of 10-15 minutes every hour. Once a week take a full day off. This hiking routine prevents injuries due to fatigue.

How do I know I'm not lost?

It's not easy to get lost. Just follow the trail markers all the way. A few simple rules of thumb: If you don't see trail markers for more than 5 minutes, look for one. There are very few reasons for not spotting a trail marker: Either you took a wrong turn, you missed a few markers because you were enjoying the view, or a few markers were covered by spring blossoms. If you can't find the markers, go back to the last place you saw one, look at the map, and make sure you know where you are.

Your backpack and what it holds

Every experienced hiker is aware of the problems associated with carrying too much weight. After all, you cannot carry less than 4-5 liters/day of water on hot days, and food is important too. Reducing the weight of your fully loaded backpack becomes a matter of packing a small toothpaste, a small bar of soap or only half of one, or using ultra light gear. The first rule is: Make sure your backpack is as light as possible. The second rule is: Don't make it too heavy. The third rule: Oh well, it's the same as the first two. **Folding knives** are not allowed. They will be confiscated by police officers if found. A list of suggested gear can be found here:

http://israeltrail.myfastforum.org/about74.html

National holidays in Israel

Most stores and supermarkets are closed on Saturdays and holidays. On Fridays and holiday eves, stores are open until 2-3 p.m. Restaurants, coffee shops, cinemas, theaters and shopping centers outside cities and towns are open on Saturdays and holidays except on Yom Kippur, when everything is closed. Below is a list of holidays during which most stores are closed:

Holiday	*2011*	*2012*	*2013*
Passover	April 19- 25	April 7 -13	Mar 26 – Apr 1
Independence day	May 9	April 26	April 16
Shavuot	June 8	May 27	May 15
Rosh Hashanah	Sept 29, 30	Sept. 17, 18	Sept 5, 6
Yom Kippur	October 8	September 26	Sept. 14
Sukkot	October 13-20	October 1-8	Sept 19-26

Insurance

Don't leave home without it, it's not just your AMEX, but more important it is your **Medical Insurance**. Make sure it covers every emergency. In case of an accident or any other mishap, contact the police by dialing **100** (police). If necessary they will alert an emergency rescue unit. Please make sure that all such eventualities, including transportation to hospitals, are covered by your medical insurance.

Weather

For the daily weather forecast in Israel check: http://www.israelweather.co.il

Money issues

Credit cards are accepted almost everywhere. For some services you have to pay cash: Taxis, a few B&Bs and some low-cost accommodations. Withdrawing cash is mostly from ATMs. If for some reason the ATM doesn't accept your credit card and you are in a town or city, look for a bank or a post office. Daily exchange rates can be found here:

http://www.bankisrael.gov.il/eng.shearim

Cell phones and emergency calls

US cell phones can be used overseas if they are quad-band GSM phones. Ask your service provider. It's cost effective to rent a cell phone overseas, where incoming calls are free, and you have prepaid minutes while traveling. If you have rented a cellular phone with rechargeable minutes, make sure you have sufficient minutes before you start hiking. If you don't bring your cellular phone, you can rent one at the airport. Two cellular phone companies have customer care service at the airport: Pelephone and Cellcom. Both are open 24/7 and are located beyond the customs area. In case of emergency call **100** (police).

Hospitals: Tiberias (Poriya): 04-665221, Zfat (Ziv) 04-6828811, Jerusalem (Hadassa) 02-6777222 or Shaarei Zedek 02-6555111.

From Ben-Gurion airport to Nazareth

Take a train (05:00-23:20 every 40 minutes to Tel Aviv), bus, or taxi to Tel Aviv, or a train to Haifa. From Tel Aviv central bus station to Nazareth, take bus number 823 or 826. From Haifa central train station, bus number 331 to Nazareth. From Haifa's Lev Hamifratz train station, take bus number 332 to Nazareth. For train schedules and fares, check at: http://www.rail.co.il/EN. For bus schedules: http://www.bus.co.il and click the English tab. There is no bus or train service on Saturdays and holidays.

Taxi: When you take a taxi always ask the driver to turn on the meter. It is cheaper than a fixed-price ride. You should only settle on a fixed rate for long distances of over 30 km. For taxi within Nazareth contact : 04-6555105, 04-6081000 or 04-6555536.

No litter policy

A no-litter policy is enforced in nature preserves. Disposing of garbage is allowed only where litter collection tanks are available. Take your litter with you. Get rid of your garbage when you get to a place with litter collection tanks.

Short dictionary

East - Mizrach. **West –** Ma'arav. **North -** Tzafon. **South -** Darom.
Right – Yemin. **Left -** Smol . **Straight -** Yashar

Be'er – Well (of water)
Biq'a – Valley
Biq'at – Valley of
Ein – Spring (of water)
Falafel – Pita bread with fried balls of chickpeas, vegetables and tahini.
Gadol – Large
Giv'a – Hill
Halva – Sweet confection based on tahini (sesame paste). Contains a lot of energy ~600 Kcal/100 grams
Har - Mountain

Hirba (Arabic word, used in Hebrew) – Ruin of an ancient or old place

Hirbot – Plural of Hirba

Hummus – Made of chickpeas, lemon juice, and garlic

Kama Ze Ole? – How much does it cost?

Kama? – Abbreviation of Kama Ze Ole?

Kfar – Village

Qatan – Small

Ma'ale – Ascent

Me'ara – Cave

Me'arot - Caves

Mitzpe – Observation point

Nahal – Creek, stream. In the desert: Dry streambed, arroyo.

Nahar - River

Pita – Pita bread

Rama – Plateau

Shalom – Peace, hi, goodbye

Shvil – Trail

Tel – A mound. Usually it is a site of the remains of ancient settlement.

Toda – Thank you

Tzomet – Road crossing

Tzuk – Cliff

Day 1: A Day in Nazareth

Map: Old city of Nazareth.

Luke 1:26-27: In the sixth month the angel Gabriel was sent from God to a city of Galilee named Nazareth, to a virgin betrothed to a man whose name was Joseph, of the house of David. And the virgin's name was Mary.

Nazareth is not cited in either the Old Testament or the Talmud. Josephus Flavius, a 1st century Romano-Jewish historian, referred to Sepphoris in his writings but made no mention of Nazareth. It must have been a small and unimportant place at the time. Nathanael asked Philip, John *1:46: "Nazareth? Can anything good come from there?"* There were good geographical reasons for his question. The ancient Via Maris linking Syria and Egypt passed east of Mount Tabor and about 10 miles east of Nazareth.

Today Nazareth is the largest Arab city in Israel, with more than 70,000 inhabitants (2010), 70% of them Moslems and 30% Christians. Nazareth is an economic, political and cultural center for the Arabs in Israel. Nearby Natzeret Illit is mostly Jewish, with more than 40,000 inhabitants. The main tourist attractions are located in the old city of Nazareth. The streets of Nazareth are numbered.

The Basilica of Annunciation

Many grottoes and wine and olive presses dating from the Stone Age have been found in the area of the Basilica of Annunciation, proving that the district was inhabited during that period, and
people engaged in agriculture. The Basilica of Annunciation is built over several ancient churches, the earliest dating from the 4th century, and reported by a pilgrim from Piacenza at about 570 CE. The second church was built during the Crusader era but was never completed. In 1739, under Ottoman rule, a new church was constructed. This church was completely demolished in 1954 to allow for the construction of the current basilica, which was completed in 1969. The main entrance is decorated with sculptures representing scenes from the Old and New Testaments. It is the

largest church in the Middle East. Its dome is 55 meters high. Open daily from 08:00-17:00.

The Synagogue Church

Isaiah 61(1):"The Spirit of the Sovereign Lord is on me, because the Lord has anointed me to proclaim good news to the poor. He has sent me to bind up the brokenhearted, to proclaim freedom for the captives and release from darkness for the prisoners."

The Synagogue Church stands at the site where, according to tradition, Jesus stood to proclaim the words of the prophet Isaiah. It was built during the Crusader period and since 1771 the Greek Catholics have taken care of it. The church is located just a few minutes walk into the old market. Open: Mon-Sat: 09:00-12:30; Mon, Tue, Thu, Fri 14:00-18:00. Sun - closed.

Mensa Christi Church

In the 17th century visiting pilgrims left marks on the rock where, according to tradition, Jesus ate with his disciples after the Resurrection. The huge rock is now located inside the church. Initially the Franciscans built a chapel at the site at the end of the 18th century, but it was rebuilt in 1861 in its present form. The church is not open for regular visits but the keys are with a family living across from the church. They will be glad to give you the key. A small gratuity is welcome. The church is located on 6126 street.

The White Mosque

The White Mosque, located in the center of the Old City, is the oldest Mosque in Nazareth. It was built in the early 19th century. The building was funded by Egyptian ruler Suleiman Pasha and its construction was supervised by Sheikh Abdulla Al-Fahum. Sheikh Abdulla chose white to represent purity, light, and peace between the various faiths of Nazareth. His tomb can be seen in the courtyard of the mosque, Old photos of Nazareth are on display in the mosque.

Mount Precipice

Luke 4:29-30: "And they rose up and drove him out of the town and brought him to the brow of the hill on which their town was built, so that they could throw him down the cliff. But passing through their midst, he went away."

Mount Precipice is located south of Nazareth, overlooking the Jezreel valley and Mount Tabor. It can be reached by taxi or on foot. If you prefer, you can visit Mount Precipice at the end of day 12.

Nazareth Village

Based on New Testament scholarship and the most up-to-date archaeology, Nazareth Village brings to life a farm and a Galilean village, recreating Nazareth as it was 2,000 years ago in the time of Jesus. Come and meet the people and experience first-century hospitality. Step through a stone doorway into the dim interior and smell the smoke from the oil lamps. Tel: 04-6456042 www.nazarethvillage.com.

The Market

The Nazareth Market is adjacent to the Basilica of the Annunciation. Experience the colors of the fruit market and the aroma of spices. Here you can purchase a variety of religious and other souvenirs. On weekends the market becomes even more vivid when merchants from the Galilee arrive to sell their merchandise. On the edge of the Old City, not far from Mary's well, is the Galilee Mill or El-Babour. The mill was built by the Wagner family of the Templar movement at the end of the 19th century to provide grinding and storage services for the city's farmers. The store has over 1000 species of spices and herbs.

Other attractions and tourist information

For all other attractions, accommodations and restaurants, please visit www.nazarethinfo.org.

Day 2: Nazareth to Cana - 15 km

Maps: Old City of Nazareth, map 1, 2. Water 2-3 liters, refill in Zippori and in Mashad.

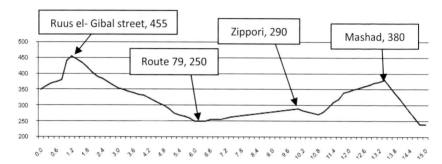

A visit to ancient Zippori is recommended. Allow at least 2 hours. If you wish to return from Zippori National Park to Nazareth, you can do so by taxi. From Mashad junction you can take a bus back to Nazareth.

Start the day at the Basilica of the Annunciation (0.0, 350). From the Basilica enter the market and go up 6152 street. The trail is marked with orange dots. Turn right by the white mosque (0.3, 360) onto 6133 street. Turn left onto 6112 street (0.4, 370). After a mild ascent continue on 6126 street. Pass the Mensa Christi Church (0.8, 380). The ascent becomes steep when you climb the steps that end on 5004 street, the Salesian Street (1.0, 440). Turn left and continue the ascent, passing the Salesian Sisters monastery on your left (1.1, 450). The trail markers are now the regular ones. At the top of the ascent turn right (1.2, 455) and you will see a panoramic view extending south to Haifa. Continue hiking on Ruus el-Gibal street and at a roundabout turn left on 7106 street down into Reina (2.1, 390). Turn left at a street fork, continue down the street, and exit Reina (3.2, 350). Continue on a 4X4 dirt road and the trail arrives at route 700 (5.6, 270) and goes down on its left shoulder. Cross route 79 (6.0, 250) and continue north on a dirt road that passes through an agricultural area. After a short ascent arrive at a paved road (9.7, 280). On your left is the gate of Zippori National Park (9.9, 290).

Zippori (Sepphoris) National Park

April to September: 08:00-17:00, October to March: 08:00-16:00, Fee. There is a snack bar, picnic area and restrooms. Tel: 04-6568272.

When Herod the Great was consolidating his power over the country early in his reign (37 BCE), Zippori fell to him without a battle. After Herod's death (4 BCE) a rebellion broke out against the Romans, but it was quelled when Zippori was destroyed by the Roman governor Varus. Herod Antipas restored the town so beautifully that Josephus Flavius described it as "the ornament of all Galilee." Later, Rabbi Judah Hanassi moved the Sanhedrin from Bet She'arim to Zippori, where he redacted the Mishnah in 220 CE. The sages of Zippori also contributed to the Jerusalem Talmud, which was completed in the 4th century CE. Christians and Jews lived together here from the 5th century on. The presence of a small Jewish community during the middle Ages is indicated by a letter found in the Cairo in the 10th century. The Crusaders believed that Ann and Joachim, the parents of Mary, mother of Jesus, lived here. Remains of the church they built commemorating St. Ann can still be seen.

A Crusader fortress, rebuilt in the 18th century by Daher al-Omar, the Bedouin ruler of the Galilee, stands at the top of a hill. The village at that time was called Safouriyeh. The 4,500-seat Roman theatre, which has been partially restored, affords a beautiful view of the Galilee Mountains and the Beit Netofa valley. Other attractions include a Talmudic-era residential quarter; the Crusader fortress; the restored 3rd century villa housing a magnificent mosaic depicting scenes from the life of Dionysus, the god of wine; and the hauntingly beautiful "Mona Lisa of the Galilee." The synagogue with its magnificent mosaic and the Nile Mosaic from the 5th century CE are also highlights, as is the 250-meter-long, 1st century CE underground water system, with a capacity of 5,000 cubic meters.

After the visit take the trail straight and east from the gate, and a few hundred meters further on the Jesus Trail joins the Israel National Trail (INT) (10.3, 260). The markers are now red. Make a right turn onto a mild ascent (11.0, 270) in a grove of pine trees. Arrive at a dirt road and turn left (11.8, 340), and climb to Mashad. By the cemetery turn left (13.5, 380) and at the main mosque the INT goes right but you turn left and down on Jesus Trail (13.7, 360). *If you want to return to Nazareth by bus, turn right on the INT and hike down until you arrive at the Mashad crossing.* Continue down and east and exit Mashad (14.3, 300) among olive groves in the direction of Cana. Arrive at the main street of Cana (14.8, 240). Turn left and after about 100 meters make a right turn into an alley (14.9, 240) and continue past the sun dial toward the Wedding Church (15.4, 230).

Cana (modern name Kafr Kanna) is a Galilean town five miles northeast of Nazareth. Its population of 8,500 includes both Muslims and Christians. Long revered as the site of Jesus' first miracle of turning water into wine at a wedding, Kafr Kanna has historical support for its authenticity as ancient Cana. The Catholic Encyclopedia of 1914, in a tradition dating back to the 8th century, identifies Cana with the town of Kafr Kana. A few recent scholars have suggested alternatives, including the village of Kenet-el-Jalil, also known as Khirbet Kana, a few kilometers further north.

The Franciscan Wedding Church at Cana was built in 1881. It is fronted by a courtyard. The facade has angel figures and is flanked by two bell towers over an arcaded narthex. Inside, the church is on two levels. The upper church has a chapel surmounted by a simple dome. In the nave just before the stairs is a fragment of a Byzantine mosaic dating from the 5th century that preserves the name of the donor in Aramaic: "In memory of the pious Joseph, son of Tanhum, son of Bota and of his children who made this table, may it be for them a blessing, Amen." The lower church has a chapel and a small museum with artifacts from the site, including a winepress, a plastered cistern and vessels of various dates. One old jar is said to be one of the six used for the miracle. Open: Mon-Sat 08:00-12:00; 14:00-18:00. Sun closed.

Opposite the Franciscan church is a beautiful Greek Orthodox Church, which is usually closed. Two 13th century capitals are displayed nearby.

Spend the night at the Cana guest house, located minutes from the Wedding Church. Tel: 04-651-7186 – Sami. www.canaguesthouse.com.

Day 3: Cana to Lavi - 17 km

Maps: 2, 3. Water: 4 liters, refill at the Golani junction.

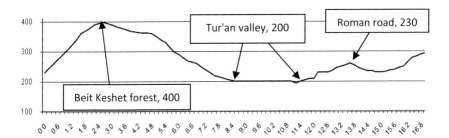

From the Golani junction you can return to Nazareth by bus. There is a MacDonald's at the Golani junction.

Start the day in Cana (0.0, 230) climb east and exit the village (1.6, 360). The paved road turns into a dirt road. You are now hiking in the Beit Keshet forest reserve. The trail turns slightly right (2.6, 400). Arrive at a paved road which is a green trail and turn left (4.8, 360). Go down along the paved road and turn left on a red trail (5.4, 330). The trail narrows and descends overlooking the beautiful Tur'an valley. Leave the red trail after a few hundred meters and turn right and east (5.7, 300). Continue until you reach the paved road that you left earlier (6.7, 260). Turn left and continue along the road. **The Gospel trail** is planned to join here from the right coming down from Mt. Precipice. The Gospel trail is an initiative of the Israel ministry of tourism. The trail markers are now green. In a pine grove on your right is a small picnic area with a few tables (7.6, 220). The area was dedicated in honor of the queen of Holland.

Turn right, and the paved road turns into a dirt road. Cross another paved road and on your left is a small snack bar (8.6, 200). *The sandwiches and prices are excellent. Joshua is the owner. Open: Sun-Thu 07:00-19:00.* The markers are orange now. Continue east on a dirt road and turn left along an old road with old electrical poles dating from the 50's (10.4, 200). Pass by a pumping station, the trail turns right toward route 65, and you cross the road using the underpass (11.2, 195). East of route 65 turn left on a black trail in a grove of eucalyptus trees. The black trail makes a sharp turn right, and you continue straight on a very mild ascent, arriving at a gas station (12.0, 210) by route 77 (water & restrooms). At the gas station turn left towards an underpass to cross route 77. After the underpass the markers are red.

At the Golani junction, a few hundred meters to the west (left) of the underpass, you can visit the Golani Memorial Museum. The Golani brigade, established on February 22, 1948, has taken part in all of Israel's wars. The museum is open Sun-Thu 09:00-16:00; Fri 09:00-13:00. The displays are in Hebrew. There is a MacDonald's next to the entrance to the museum.

At the exit from the underpass turn right and make an immediate left turn onto a mild ascent on the red trail. At the top of the ascent you will arrive at the remains of an ancient Roman road (12.5, 230).

The Roman road linked Acre on the Mediterranean with Tiberias on the Sea of Galilee. Route 77 in the Tur'an valley parallels the ancient Roman road. Another good example of a modern road that follows a similar path to a Roman road is the one from Ashkelon on the Mediterranean to Jerusalem. Distances on Roman roads were measured by milestones. Several milestones from the Roman era can still be seen on the ancient road from Ashkelon to Jerusalem. The Romans utilized a vast network of roads to control and protect their empire. The main roads were for public and military use. There were also private and agricultural roads, and the regional roads were dirt roads. The road here is of the first type.

Turn right and east and hike toward Kibbutz Lavi. You will hike next to a power line (13.2, 260). Turn right away from the power line (14.2, 240) and after a short and very mild descent arrive at Lavi cemetery and a Holocaust memorial (15.0, 230). There is water in the cemetery.

The Holocaust memorial commemorates the parents and relatives of members of Kibbutz Lavi, which is a religious community established in 1949 by young immigrants mostly from the UK. They were refugees from Nazi Germany who were part of the Kindertransport, a rescue mission undertaken shortly before the Second World War to save Jewish children from the Nazis. The UK took in almost 10,000 children.

To get to the Illaniya B&B turn right by the cemetery and hike south until you reach route 77. Contact the Illaniya B&B from the Lavi junction and make sure they will pick you up. The Lavi hotel is on the grounds of the kibbutz. If you prefer you can camp in the area or in the Lavi forest in a designated camping area east of the Golani junction.

Turn left from the cemetery to the north. Turn right and east (15.6, 240) and go uphill, crossing a gate in a cattle fence, until the trail passes by the rear gate of the kibbutz (16.7, 290). Turn right onto the road that leads to the hotel. There are signs pointing to the hotel. Kibbutz Lavi is a Jewish religious community.

Day 4: Lavi to Moshav Arbel - 15 km

Map 4. Water 4 liters, refill in Nabi Shua'yb.

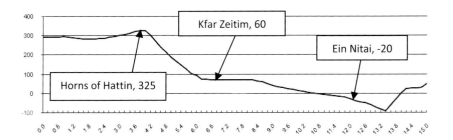

If you spend the night in Illaniya B&B ask the owner to drop you off at the rear gate of Kibbutz Lavi, which is not far from the Lavi hotel. There is a B&B in Kfar Zeitim and in Moshav Arbel.

Start the day at the rear gate of kibbutz Lavi (0.0, 290). From the gate take a dirt road that joins the trail by the Lavi dairy farm or go back to the trail and continue northeast passing under a power line (0.7, 295). Turn right (1.5, 280) and after passing the Lavi dairy farm turn left (1.8, 280). Pass a cattle guard and turn right onto a black trail (2.3, 285). Continue east on a mild ascent towards the Horns of Hattin. Pass a cattle grid and when you meet a blue trail turn left at the foot of the Horns of Hattin. Climb the hill on your left for a magnificent panorama of the area (4.0, 325).

On July 4th, 1187 Saladin of the Ayyubid dynasty fought and defeated the Crusader Kingdom of Jerusalem under the leadership of Guy of Lusignan and Raymond III of Tripoli. One day earlier the Crusaders had left Zippori to face Saladin's advance forces. At midday they arrived at the village of Tur'an, where water was available, Guy had decided to march towards the town of Tiberias, that had been taken by Saladin. The Crusaders could not cover the distance of 14 km due to continuous attacks by Saladin's cavalry. Lacking water and supplies, they were forced to stop in the area of Hattin. The next day they were defeated and suffered very heavy casualties. Most of the Crusaders, some 17,000 in all, lost their lives, while Saladin's forces suffered only minor loses. Guy of Lusignan was captured along with several other leaders. He was brought to Syria and released the following year.

Mount Arbel and the Arbel valley are visible to the east from the Horns of Hattin. Continue northwest on a blue trail. The trail goes down on a steep and rocky descent that becomes moderate for a short distance (4.4, 270). The trail veers until it arrives at the entry road to Nabi Shua'yb (5.2, 165). Turn left to visit the holy site.

Nabi Shu'ayb (The prophet Jethro), is a central figure in the Druze religion. The tomb of Nabi Shu'ayb has been a site of annual pilgrimage for the Druze for centuries. The first mention of the tomb dates back to the 12th century CE, and the Druze have held religious festivals there for centuries. According to Druze tradition, the imprint of Shuayb's left foot (da'sa) can be seen on the grave. Pilgrims visiting the site pour oil into the imprint, and then rub the oil over their body in order to be blessed with good fortune. The Druze customarily had no fixed date for their annual pilgrimage, which generally occurred sometime in the spring. When the Israeli government granted official recognition of the pilgrimage as a Druze religious holiday, the dates were standardized, and the event now takes place between April 25 and April 28. During the festivities, mass celebrations are held at Nabi Shu'ayb, and Druze religious leaders gather there for ritual purposes and to discuss religious questions.

The five-colored Druze flag was designed to distinguish the Druze Islamic sect from other sects. There are many interpretations for this flag, but the main one is that it represents Fatimah, her father (Muhammad), her husband, and her two sons. Other interpretations of the five colors are: Red is for courage, bravery and love. Yellow is knowledge, wisdom, enlightenment and wheat. Green is nature and earth. Blue signifies patience, forgiveness, sky and water. White is purity, peace and conciliation.

Nabi Shu'ayb has been expanded and renovated over time. The older section of the existing structure was built in the 1880s, after the spiritual leader of the Druze, Sheikh Muhammad Tarif, summoned an assembly of religious leaders in the community to collaborate on its construction. A delegation of high-ranking community members traveled to Syria and Lebanon to collect funds for the new construction and renovations, and the Druze of the Galilee and Mount Carmel also made considerable contributions. The chandelier in the central convention hall was designed in Syria, the glass came from Egypt, and the construction was completed by experts from Jordan.

From Nabi Shua'yb continue on the paved road (turn right when coming down from the IIorns of Hattin) east and at route 7717 turn left toward Kfar Zeitim (6.2, 75). *In Kfar Zeitim there is a B&B.* At the entrance to Kfar Zeitim (6.6, 70) continue straight on a blue trail which is dirt road, next to an olive grove. On you left you will see the ruins of the Arab village of Hittin. Make a right turn where a black trail joins from the left (8.2, 70). There is an impressive view of Mount Arbel and Mount Nitai to the east. Continue on a very mild descent along Nahal Nimerim. When you come to a fork in the dirt road make a left turn and you will pass a pumping station, Hittim (חיטים) number 3 (8.9, 40). Cross a cattle guard and arrive at another fork in the dirt road. A black trail comes from your left, and you make a right turn and continue on the blue trail (10.6, 0), you are at sea level now.

Cross a cattle guard and arrive at Ein Nitai (11.7, -20). This small and lovely spring is the perfect place for a break. Continue east along Nahal Arbel on the gravel road, passing few large eucalyptus trees (12.2, -40). A few hundred meters further along Nahal Arbel you will see a huge mulberry tree. Cross Nahal Arbel a few times and at the entrance to the Arbel Nature Reserve by an abandoned building (13.3, -90) make a right turn to begin the steep ascent toward Moshav Arbel. **The Gospel Trail** is planned to continue here down in Nahal Arbel. The blue trail ends above sea level at the entry road to Moshav Arbel (14.1, 25). Turn left and then turn right and follow a green trail that brings you to the ancient Arbel Synagogue (14.8, 30), that dates back to the 4th century CE. To reach Moshav Arbel take the trail that goes south from the Synagogue into Moshav Arbel (15.3, 50). *You can camp in the area.*

Day 5: Moshav Arbel to Tabgha - 15 km

Maps: 5, 6. Water 4 liters, refill in Migdal.

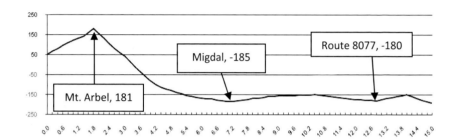

Start the day at the road to Mount Arbel, on the north side of Moshav Arbel (0.0, 50). Climb east and arrive at Mt. Arbel Park (fee) (1.5, 150). If you start early enough you can watch the sun rise over the Golan Heights and the Sea of Galilee (Kinneret). Take the black trail that leads to the top of the cliff (1.8, 181). The view towards the Kinneret, some 400 meters below, is magnificent. Mount Nitai is opposite, on the other side of the deep valley which was formed by volcanic activity.

The name Kinneret was mentioned as early as 1450 BCE by Thutmose the 3rd as one of the places he captured during his reign. The word Kinneret is derived from the Canaanite language. Later, in the Talmudic period (300-400 CE), it was known as the "Sea of Tiberias," a name which is used in Arabic بحيرة طبريا (Buheirat Tabria) and in French "Le lac de Tibériade". The Latin Name "Mare Galilaeae" is similar to the Sea of Galilee.

Descend from Mt. Arbel on the black trail that follows the path of the Israel National Trail (INT). Metal handles and cables assist you on the way down. You will pass by the Arbel Fort.

The site was inhabited as early as the Stone Age. The natural caves were expanded to include water cisterns. During the Hasmonean revolt (167-161 BCE) against Antiochus the 4th Epiphanes, the caves were used as a hiding place. The soldiers of King Herod (74-4 BCE) chased the Kanaim (Zealot) rebels who hid here.. Herod's soldiers lowered baskets from the cliff top to gain entry to the caves. During the great Jewish Revolt (66-70 CE) the Kanaim rebels in the Galilee also made use of the caves until the Romans, led by Vespasian (9-79 CE) and succeeded by his son Titus (39-81 CE), ended the revolt and destroyed the Second Temple (70 CE). The Arbel Fort dates back to the 17th century, when it was used by the Druze in their revolt against the Ottoman rulers.

Continue the descent until you link up with the red trail (2.9, 40) that goes down from the west side of the Arbel cliff; you are now hiking below sea level. Arrive at Hamam, a Bedouin village of the Awarna tribe (4.5, -115). *The original families lived in 13 small villages further north in the Hula valley. In 1948 they were moved here. There is a grocery store in Hamam.* Continue towards the exit from Hamam and cross route 807 by the gas station (5.7, -165). Continue north to Migdal. Pass a small supermarket by the main entrance road to Migdal (7.1, -185). Continue north on the INT. Pass Ein Nun - the Nun spring, which is a lovely place for a break. A blue trail crosses the INT (8.7, -160).

The INT turns left into Nahal Amud on a black trail (10.3, -150). To the right the black trail leads to the Sea of Galilee. Continue on the orange-marked Jesus Trail. Arrive at route 8077 that goes west to Hukok and Livnim (12.7, -180). There is a gas station on the north side of the road. At route 90 turn left and north and continue the hike uphill. The dirt road crosses route 90 to its east side (14.0, -150). Use caution when crossing the busy highway. After you cross route 90 turn left and go down. The trail crosses the access road to Pilgerhaus Tabgha (14.5, -190). *It was established in 1889 by the Lazarists, whose goal, apart from pilgrimage, was to train local Bedouins in agriculture. After 1948 the site was confiscated, and in the 1990's it was returned to the German Association for the Holy Land.* Arrive at Tabgha (14.9, -190).

There are several places to stay in the area: Migdal, Tamar camping site, Pilgerhaus Tabgha, the Mount of Beatitudes Guesthouse (2 minutes by bus from Tabgha + 0.75 km walk from the road, or hike north and uphill from Tabgha for approx. 1.5 km), Vered Hagalil and Korazim, both less than 10 minutes by bus. Please check in Accommodations for details. Buses from the Kfar Nahum junction run every 30 minutes between 07:00-20:00 and every hour after 20:00. On Friday the buses run until 17:00.

Holy Sites on the Shore of the Sea of Galilee

Maps: 5, 6. Water 3 liters, refill in Capernaum.

If you want to visit all the holy sites on the north shore of the Sea of Galilee, it is recommended that you spend at least a day and half in the area and allow half a day rest before you continue south. On the first day you will visit the Mount of Beatitudes, Tabgha, the St. Peter Primacy Church, and Capernaum. On the second day we recommend that you visit the Domus Galilaeae in Korazim and the Jesus Boat in Ginosar. Both places can be reached by bus.

Day 6: Mount of Beatitudes to Capernaum - 12 km

There is no hiking trail from the Domus Galilaeae to the Mount of Beatitudes. The area is blocked by a barbed-wire cattle fence. Take a bus if you are not staying at the Mount of Beatitudes hostel. The buses on route 90 run every 30 minutes or so. There is a bus station on route 90, at the entry road leading to the monastery and church. From the bus station hike east and arrive at the entrance to the Mount of Beatitudes church and monastery (~1 km). The only descent of the day is from Mount of Beatitudes to Tabgha an elevation change of ~100 meters. The rest of the day is hiking along the shores of the Sea of Galilee.

Start the day on the Mount of Beatitudes (0.0, -90). After visiting the Church take a non-marked trail (dirt road) down and south toward Tabgha and the Sea of Galilee. Just before arriving at route 87 on your right there is a tiny cave with a bench (1.4, -180). Take a break and enjoy the view of the Sea of

Galilee. Go down by way of the metal stairs and carefully cross route 87 (1.5, -190). Turn right and continue on the sidewalk to Tabgha (2.0, -190). After visiting Tabgha turn back (east) and visit the Church of the Primacy of St. Peter (2.5, -190). Continue east to visit Capernaum. Turn right at the entrance road to Capernaum (4.4, -195) and arrive at a gate (5.0, -200). After visiting Capernaum return to route 87 (5.5, -195), turn right and continue east along route 87. Turn right (6.4, -195) and arrive at the lovely Twelve Apostles Greek Orthodox church (7.2, -210). Hike back to Tabgha along route 87 and arrive to route 90 (11.7, -190). Take a bus back to where you plan to spend the night.

Mount of Beatitudes

Open: Daily 08:00-11:30; 14:00-16:30. Allow up to one hour. Free.

Matthew 5:1-3: "Now when Jesus saw the crowds, he went up on a mountainside and sat down. His disciples came to him, and he began to teach them: Blessed are the poor in spirit, for theirs is the kingdom of heaven."

Located on a hill overlooking the Sea of Galilee and Tabgha, the Mount of Beatitudes is, according to tradition, the site where Jesus delivered the most famous sermon of all times: The Sermon on the Mount. It is questionable whether this is the exact location where he stood and spoke to his disciples, but considering that Jesus lived in Capernaum and the area is not mountainous, this hill is a likely site for the Sermon on the Mount. Remains of a 4th century Byzantine church have been found here. Parts of a cistern and a monastery are still visible.

In 1907 the area was purchased by the *"Associazione Nazionale per Soccorrere i Missionari Italiani"*, the National Association for Assistance to Italian Missionaries. founded in 1886. The church was built in 1938. The architect was Antonio Barluzzi (1884-1960), who designed many religious institutions in the Holy Land. The shape of the church is octagonal, to represent the eight beatitudes. The lower walls are encased in marble veneer and the dome is covered in gold mosaic. The main attraction is the cool, quiet garden overlooking the Sea of Galilee. Here, where Jesus conducted his ministry, is an excellent place to contemplate some of the best-known Christian teachings.

Tabgha and the Church of the Multiplication

Open: Mon-Fri 08:00-17:00; Sat: 08:00-15:00. Sun closed. Allow half an hour. Free.

Tabgha is traditionally believed to be the site of the miracle of the multiplication of the loaves and fishes. The story is found in all four gospels. The name is derived from the Greek *Heptapegon* ("seven springs"). A Church of the Feeding of the Five Thousand was first built here circa 350. The church was small (16m x10m) and on a slightly different orientation than the later versions. After visiting the church in the 380s, the Spanish pilgrim Egeria wrote:

"By the sea is a grassy field with plenty of hay and many palm trees. By them are seven springs, each flowing strongly. And this is the field where the Lord fed the people with the five loaves and two fishes. In fact the stone on which the Lord placed the bread has now been made into an altar. People who go there take away small pieces of the stone to bring them prosperity, and they are very effective."

The church was significantly enlarged around 480, when the splendid floor mosaic was added. The mosaics were repaired in the 6th century but the church was destroyed around 700 CE. In 1932 the site was bought and excavated by the Deutsche Verien vom Heilige Lande; a protective cover was built over the mosaics in 1936. In 1982 this was replaced by the modern Church of the Multiplication of the Loaves and Fishes that stands today and is a faithful reconstruction of the original.

Church of the Primacy of Peter

Open: Daily: 08:00-17:00. Allow half an hour. Free.

Matthew 16: 18-19: And I tell you that you are Peter and on this rock I will build my church, and the gates of Hades will not overcome it. I will give you the keys of the kingdom of heaven; whatever you bind on earth will be bound in heaven, and whatever you loose on earth will be loosed in heaven."

The Church of the Primacy of Peter is a Franciscan chapel located at Tabgha, commemorating Jesus' reinstatement of Peter. At the base of the chapel walls on the west end, the walls of the late 4th-century church are clearly visible on three sides. Like the early church, the altar of the modern chapel incorporates a large portion of the stone "table of Christ" (Latin: *Mensa Christi*). This is where Jesus is believed to have served his disciples a breakfast of fish after they landed on shore *(John 21:9)*. On the lake side of the church are the rock-cut steps mentioned by Egeria as the place "where the Lord stood."

Capernaum

Open: Daily 08:00-16:30. Allow 1 hour. Fee: NIS 3.

Matthew 4:12-13: "When Jesus heard that John had been put in prison, he returned to Galilee. Leaving Nazareth, he went and lived in Capernaum, which was by the lake in the area of Zebulun and Napthali."

The site of the ancient fishing village of Capernaum (Hebrew: *Kfar Nahum*, the Village of Nahum) is located 2.5 kilometers northeast of Tabgha. The town is first mentioned in the New Testament, where it figures prominently in the Gospel narratives as the place where Jesus lived during much of his ministry in the Galilee. It was here that Jesus "cured many who were suffering from diseases," and also "cast out many devils" in those possessed. In 381, the pilgrim Egeria said she visited *"the synagogue where the Lord cured a man possessed by a devil. The way in is up many stairs, and it is made of dressed stone."* The synagogue at Capernaum probably dates from the 4th century CE. The ornately carved, white building stones of the synagogue stand out prominently among the smaller, plain blocks of local black basalt used for the town's other buildings, which are almost all residential.

Several of the Apostles - Peter and his brother Andrew, James son of Zebedee and his brother John - lived in the village, where Matthew was a tax collector. Archeological evidence indicates that the town was established at the beginning of the Hasmonean Dynasty (the earliest coins found at the site date from the 2nd century BCE). The town, near the border of the province of Galilee, was situated on a branch of the *Via Maris* trade route. At the time of the Gospel narrative, Capernaum included a customs post and a small Roman garrison commanded by a centurion.

The church of Capernaum was founded on the traditional site of St. Peter's home. Closer to the shore than the synagogue, the house was in a poor area where the dry stone basalt walls would have supported only a light roof (which suits the lowering of the paralytic in Mark 2:1-12) and would not have had windows. The village, badly damaged by an earthquake in 746, was rebuilt a short distance to the northeast (near the present Greek Orthodox Church), but little is known of its subsequent history, decline and eventual abandonment sometime in the 11th century. Despite the importance of Capernaum in the life of Jesus, there is no indication of any construction during the Crusader period. A 13th-century traveler found only the huts of seven poor fishermen.

The site was "re-discovered" in 1838 by Dr. Edward Robinson, the American biblical geographer. In 1866, the British explorer Captain Charles W. Wilson identified the ruins of the synagogue, and in 1894 a portion of the ancient site was purchased by the Franciscan Custody of the Holy Land. The principal Franciscan excavations took place in 1968-84. In 1990, the Franciscans built the modern church over the site of St. Peter's house. Hexagonal in shape and rather spaceship-like in appearance, it is elevated on pillars and has a glass floor, so visitors can still see the original church below. In March 2000, Pope John Paul II visited Capernaum during his visit to the Holy Land.

Twelve Apostles Greek Orthodox Church

Open: Daily 08:30-17:00. Allow half an hour. Free.

The small, beautiful and picturesque Twelve Apostles Greek Orthodox Church, with its pink red dome, was constructed in 1931. The walls are decorated with huge frescoes painted by Greek artists. It is the most beautiful church in the area.

Day 7: Domus Galilaeae and Jesus Boat to Migdal - 5 km

Take a bus to Korazim junction. From route 90 hike east on route 8277. Turn right and arrive to Domus Galilaeae (0.5). After the visit return to route 90 and take a bus to Ginosar (1.0). Visit the Jesus Boat at the local museum (1.7). From Ginosar go back to route 90 (2.4, -175) and turn left and south. After approximately 300 meters turn right on a dirt road and continue west for another 300 meters, until you reach the Jesus trail (2.5, -180), which is also the INT. Turn left and south on the INT and arrive at Migdal (3.7, -185). Continue south until you arrive at the gas station on route 807 (5.1, -185). Before you continue the hike, it is important to take half a day off and rest.

Domus Galilaeae

Open: Mon-Sat: 09:00-12:00; 15:00-16:30. Sun: Closed. Guided tours only; allow up to 1 hour. Free.

The original project is by Kiko Argüello, a famous Spanish painter, and Carmen Hernandez, the initiator of the Neocatechumenal Way. The very beautiful project of Domus Galilaeae where Pope John Paul 2nd celebrated the Eucharist on March 24th, 2000 on the Mount of Beatitudes, is an attempt to rediscover architectural and iconographic shapes and help to reintroduce beauty into the life of the Church.

Construction began in January 1999 under the direction of an Israeli architect, Dan Mochly from Haifa, in collaboration with an Argentinean architect, Rev. Daniel Cevilan. The first terrace, the highest in reference to the lake, includes a congressional center, with all the facilities for simultaneous translations, and capable of accommodating 300 persons. In order to facilitate study and to deepen the understanding of Sacred Scripture, with special attention to the Sermon of the Mount, there is a computerized library for Biblical studies. The complex includes also a Church for Eucharistic celebrations and a Chapel of the Blessed Sacrament surmounted by a stylish chalice which refers to the passion of Christ.

The Jesus Boat museum

Open: Sun-Thu 08:00-17:00; Fri 08:00-16:00; Sat 08:00-16:00. Fee.

On January 24th, 1986, a historic archaeological discovery was made on the Galilee lake shore at Kibbutz Ginosar. The discovery rocked the world of faith, history and archaeology. Following a prolonged drought that had lowered the sea level of the lake, two fisherman brothers discovered an ancient boat. In Israel, a land blessed with a rich history and hundreds of thousands of artifacts, important discoveries occur on a fairly regular basis. This discovery was different however; there must have been something more to the story.

Experts from all over the world were brought in to establish the boat's authenticity and exact age by means of scientific methods, including three independent precision Carbon-14 dating examinations that determined the boat is dated to the time of Jesus. The boat might conceivably have been used by Jesus or one of his disciples for fishing and transportation. Word of the unprecedented discovery traveled rapidly throughout the scientific community, and to people of faith around the world. What had been found was a Bible-era artifact like no other. Some consider it to be among the top ten biblical archaeological discoveries ever made. The Jesus Boat is a one-of-a-kind actual point of contact with the exact time and place of Jesus.

Day 8: Migdal to Poriya - 18 km.

Maps: 7, 8. Drinking water: 4 liters, refill in Mizpe.

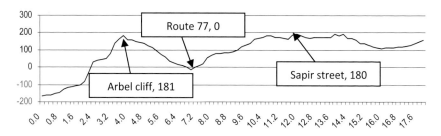

Start on route 807 by the gas station south of Migdal (0.0, -165). Go east and make a left turn southwest to Hamam. After ~1.5 km a red trail goes up to Mt. Arbel (1.5, -115). It's a steep climb that takes you from ~120m below sea level to ~180m above. The red trail goes up and splits halfway to the top (2.5, 40). Take the left branch on a black trail and continue the ascent. Metal handles and cables assist you on the way up. Arrive at the top of Mt. Arbel (3.5, 165). Take a break at the top of Mt. Arbel (181), and enjoy once more the view of the Kinneret and the Golan heights. After the break continue east and south on the Israel National Trail (INT) towards Kfar Hittim. Before arriving at Kfar Hittim pass by the village cemetery (6.5, 10). Hike on the east side of the village along its fence. Make a right turn down and at a 4X4 dirt road make another right turn onto a green trail. The green trail leads to route 7717 (7.2, 0). Make a left turn east and after 300 m along route 7717, make a right turn south and go up to Mizpe. In Mizpe reach route 77. Hike along route 77 for 300 m and then cross it to a gas station and a small supermarket (9.0, 90). In the supermarket you will see a notebook in which hikers leave remarks and comments when they pass through here. *If you want to visit Tiberias there are buses on route 77 going down to Tiberias.*

Continue climbing south up Sapir Avenue in Tiberias Illit for about 1.5 km, where the INT leaves Tiberias Illit and goes south through a forest reserve. There is a trail sign here (10.5, 180). Continue through the reserve with its stunning panorama of the Kinneret and the Golan Heights. At a trail fork a blue trail goes down and left (13.5, 175). Continue on the INT until you arrive at route 7677 (17.0, 120). *If you're spending the night in Poriya Illit B&B, make a right turn west and climb on route 7677 to Poriya (18.4, 160). If you're spending the night at Poriya Guest House, go down along route 7677 and after the second hairpin bend, take the trail north to the guest house (18.0, 60).*

Day 9: Poriya to Yavne'el - 18 km

Maps: 8, 9. Drinking water: 4 liters. Refill in Yardenit.

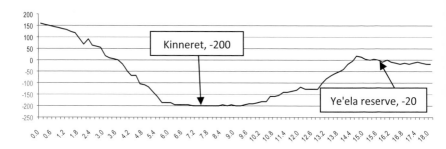

The distance between Yardenit and Kfar Kish is too long for one day for the average hiker (27 km). If you stop at Yardenit for a visit you won't be able to cover the distance. I'll take you to Yavne'el even though it's off trail. You can skip the detour to Yavne'el and camp in the area where the black trail meets the red one at kilometer 15.0 or in Hirbat Ulam at kilometer 9.9 of day 10. **In that case make sure you have at least 7 liters of water when you leave Yardenit Baptismal site.** *The following water refill is in Kfar Kish, which is 27 kilometers from Yardenit.*

From Poriya Illit (0.0, 160) go down on route 7677 (1.5, 120). Arrive at the INT and make a right turn south. *From Poriya Guest House go south, until you arrive at route 7677.* After a trail fork (2.1, 110) the INT turns left on a short and moderate descent (2.6, 60). Pass through a cattle gate (2.8, 55) and turn left by a memorial that commemorates 80 years of Kinneret village (3.5, 0). Continue the descent, once again below sea level. You will pass an olive grove, palm trees, a fence (4.7, -110), and a power line further down. Arrive in the Moshava (village) of Kinneret and Ha'meyasdim Street (5.5, -185). *The village was established in 1908. The poetess Rachel (1890-1931), one of Israel's most famous poets, is buried in the local cemetery.*

At the end of Ha'meyasdim street turn left (6.0, -185) and continue towards Kinneret junction. Turn right at the junction (6.2, -200). After passing a grove of palm trees turn right. Continue south and pass a small memorial for the Mule Buba (doll) (6.8, -195). Pass an old pumping station - the Motor

House, (7.5, -200) and take a left turn to the road that leads to the **Yardenit Baptismal Site on the Jordan River.**

Mark 1, 9-11: "At that time Jesus came from Nazareth in Galilee and was baptized by John in the Jordan. Just as Jesus was coming up out of the water, he saw heaven being torn open and the Spirit descending on him like a dove. And a voice came from heaven: You are my Son, whom I love; with you I am well pleased".

Open: March to November: Sun-Thu 08:00-18:00 Fri to 14:00. December to February: Sun-Thu 08:00-17:00 Fri 08:00-14:00. Yardenit is closed only on Yom Kippur. Tel: 04-6759111. In Yardenit there is a restaurant and restrooms.

After the visit of Yardenit continue the hike and pass the Motor House, make a right turn, and after 200 meters turn left onto a blue trail. Continue south along the west bank of the Jordan River. Pass the Rob Roy canoeing site (8.3, -200). The blue trail makes a left turn east (9.0, -200), and you continue south on the INT. *There is a grocery store in Degania B (1 km from here).* Continue south under a power line. Arrive at a trail crossing (9.8, -190). A black trail goes right and you continue straight on the INT. Arrive at a trail crossing, turn right and west onto a green trail (10.3, -180) and hike on the green trail above Nahal Yavne'el. Cross under a power line (10.9, -155) and a pumping station (12.0, 120), and continue the mild ascent. At a trail crossing (12.8, -125), turn right onto a black trail and start a moderate ascent that becomes difficult at times. If you continue west on the green trail along the scenic Nahal Yavne'el you will arrive at Yavne'el after another 4 kilometers (17.0, -20). Continue the climb on the black trail. Arrive at a trail crossing with a dirt road (15.0, 10). Turn right and west on the red trail and hike toward Yavne'el. Arrive in the industrial zone off Yavne'el (18.0, 20). *On the east side of the village, off route 767, there is private camping. B&B is also available in Yavne'el.* Tel Yin'am is located near the Yavne'el camping site. The name is derived from the Arabic Tel a-Na'am. It has been identified as the site of biblical Yavne'el (see Joshua 19:33). Excavations have revealed that Tel Yin'am was continually inhabited from the Neolithic period to the end of the Byzantine period making it a likely site for an overnight stop when travelling between Capernaum and Mt. Tabor. Notable discoveries include the image of a Canaanite goddess made of electrum, an alloy of gold and silver, and an installation for smelting iron which dates back to the 13th century BCE. This appears to be the most ancient iron smelting plant in the Holy Land.

Day 10: Yavne'el to Kfar Kish - 21 km

Maps: 9, 10. Water: 5 liters. Refill of water is not possible on the way.

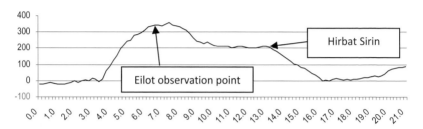

Start on the red trail southeast of Yavne'el (0.0, -20). If you pass the local stadium you're going in the wrong direction. Hike on the red trail east. Arrive at the black trail (3.5, 20), turn right and south, and climb towards the Eilot Observation Point. It's a steep ascent. Arrive at a dirt road (4.0, 85) and continue for ~300 meters before leaving the dirt road (4.3, 155). A sign marks the limits of Eilot Nature Preserve (4.6, 195). Enjoy the view from the Eilot Observation Point: you can see the Golan Heights on the northeast, the Jordan Valley below, and the Sea of Galilee. Continue the climb until you reach a trail junction where a blue trail goes east and down to Menahamia (6.6, 245). Leave the black trail and turn right and west on the INT (7.0, 280). After passing by a triangulation point (three metal poles) pass by a tower that the locals call "The Helicopter" (7.3, 345). It is a resting place for farmers. Turn left and south and continue the hike on a black trail. After passing the irrigation pumps on your right the black trail ends (8.0, 330).

Turn right and west on a blue trail and after about 400 m (8.4, 310) turn left and south onto a green trail. Continue on the green trail, cross Nahal Ulam and pass through an olive grove until you arrive at Hirbat Ulam (9.9, 220). **You can camp here too.** *An Arab village was built here in the 19th century on the ruins of an ancient settlement dating from the Roman Byzantine era.*

The village has been abandoned since 1948. After a break continue the mild descent on the green trail. After passing an irrigation device (10.9, 200) the trail becomes almost flat. Pass another irrigation device (12.0, 200) and turn right on a black trail (12.1, 200). Continue on the black trail and arrive at Hirbat Sirin (12.8, 210). *Here the remains of a synagogue dating from the 3rd century CE were found, and the remains of a mosque as well.* East of Hirbat Sirin the black trail turns right, goes west (13.0, 215), and passes by a fence. Continue west on a mild ascent and you will pass yet another irrigation device (13.6, 180). A green trail leads right and east (14.5, 105) and you continue west on the black trail.

Pass through a gate in a cattle fence (15.1, 75) and at a fork take the right wing and go under a power line (15.7, 35). *You will pass just north of Tel Rekesh, an ancient city mentioned by Thutmose III and his son Amenhotep II that dates back to 1500 BCE.* Continue the mild ascent and arrive at a trail crossing at sea level (16.2, 0). The black trail turns left towards Nahal Tavor and you continue west on the green trail. You pass by a water reservoir and a pumping station on your left (17.0, 15). Further west you will cross Nahal Tavor. In winter and spring you may find yourself crossing a stream of water. Hike under a power line, and the green trail ends (18.4, 15). Make a right turn west on a red trail and cross Nahal Gazit. Continue on the red trail which is a dirt road, until you arrive at route 7276 (19.5, 30). Turn right into Kfar Kish and arrive at the village center near the grocery store. (21.0, 85).

Kfar Kish is named after Brigadier General Frederick Kish. Kish was born in India in 1888 and served in the British Army during WW1. In 1923-1931 he headed the Zionist Commission in Palestine. He returned to military service in WW2 and was killed in action in Tunisia.

Camping is permitted in the area of Kfar Kish. B&B and family stay is available in the village and also in Kfar Tavor, few kilometers to the north. At Gazit junction on route 65 there is a road inn.

Day 11: Kfar Kish to Nazareth - 24 km

Maps: 10-12. Drinking water: 4-5 liters, refill in Shibli and on Mt. Tabor. If you have not yet visited Mt. Precipice you can take the alternate route from Mt. Debora to Mt. Precipice. The hike from Kfar Kish to Mt.

Precipice is approximately 30 km long, and ends on a very steep ascent. We recommend that you cover the distance over two days, spending the afternoon and a night in Shibli.

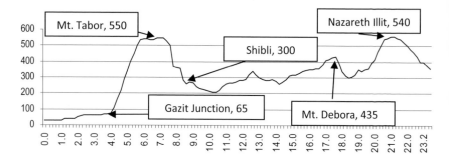

Start the day at route 7276 at the exit from Kfar Kish (0.0, 30) and go west along the road. At the junction (left to Ein Dor), the INT goes down to Nahal Tabor (1.0, 30) and continues west along the creek for about a mile., Turn right and continue along route 7276 until the INT arrives at route 65 (3.5, 65). *At the junction there is a gas station and a convenience store.* Make a left turn, cross route 65 and make a right turn west toward Shibli (3.7, 65). Hike to Shibli and after about 300 meters, make a left turn onto a blue trail up to Mt. Tabor (4.0, 75). The very steep ascent (~30% gradient) takes you to the top of Mt. Tabor. Cross three dirt roads and at the top turn left onto a black trail (5.7, 535). After approx. 400m a red trail goes left and down to Um-Ranem. Continue on the black trail and make a right turn (6.5, 535) arriving at the parking lot of the Transfiguration Church.

"Matthew 17:1-3: After six days Jesus took with him Peter, James and John the brother of James, and led them up a high mountain by themselves. There he was transfigured before them. His face shone like the sun, and his clothes became as white as the light. Just then there appeared before them Moses and Elijah, talking with Jesus."

Make a right turn into the parking lot and turn right again into the church.

Open between: 08:00-12:00; and 14:00-17:00. <u>In the monastery there are rooms for pilgrims, inquire on site (Tel: 04-6620720).</u> The church was designed by Antonio Barluzzi (1884–1960), an Italian Franciscan monk and architect, who was known as the "Architect of the Holy Land". He designed *numerous churches in the Holy Land. The Transfiguration Church was completed in 1924. In 1964 Pope Paul VI visited Mt. Tabor.*

After the visit, exit through the main gate of the monastery on the west side of Mt. Tabor. Make a right turn north onto the black trail. After approx. 400m you will pass by a Greek Orthodox Monastery (7.2, 550). Cross the road and the black trail ends. Continue on a green trail and make a left turn down to Shibli. In Shibli, at the foot of Mt. Tabor (8.4, 280), you will find a kiosk, a souvenir shop, tables, and restrooms. *There is a Kupat Holim medical center in Shibli.* Turn right and east, and at a T junction turn left and north onto a blue trail (8.6, 260). Continue on the blue trail north for ~1 km. Turn right and east (9.6, 225) on a red trail and after about half a kilometer make a left turn north onto a black trail (10.1, 205). Continue on the black trail northwest passing a cattle guard (11.2, 265) and turn right onto a blue trail (12.6, 290). After about 200 meters make another left turn onto a green trail (12.8, 320). The green trail winds southeast and arrives at an observation point facing Mt. Tabor (14.1, 260). Pass under a power line (15.5, 330) and arrive at a trail junction (15.6, 340).

Take the INT south and climb Mt. Debora. The INT makes a right turn onto a fine dirt road black trail (16.7, 380). At the top of Mt. Debora take a break (17.5, 435). *There is an excellent view of Mt. Tabor from the east side of Mt. Debora. And you will find here a memorial in honor of the 25th wedding anniversary of Queen Elizabeth II and her husband Prince Philip.* From the top take the blue trail down and north. Arrive at a road and a trail junction: black and red (18.4, 300). To arrive to Mount Precipice on a non marked trail follow the description of day 12 below. Take the red trail north up to Mt. Jona. Climb up the red trail for about 2 km. *To your right (east) is Ein Mahel. To your left (west) is the* **Nazareth Iris** *Nature Reserve. In spring you can see magnificent irises here.* Arrive at Nazareth Illit and turn right along a wall (20.6, 540). To get to Mashad continue on the INT hiking Shderot Ma'ale Yitzhak. Leave Shderot Ma'ale Yitzhak and go down and west passing a grove of olive trees. Arrive at Mashad junction (23.6, 360). *Take bus #28 to Nazareth if you plan to spend the night at* **Fauzi Azar Inn.**

Day 12: Shibli to Mount Precipice - 22 km

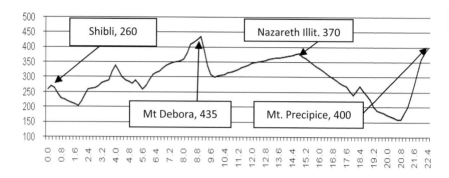

From Shibli, at the foot of Mt. Tabor (0.0, 280), turn right and east, and at a T junction turn left and north onto a blue trail (0.2, 260). Continue on the blue trail north for ~1 km. Turn right and east (1.2, 225) on a red trail and after about half a kilometer make a left turn north onto a black trail (1.7, 205). Continue on the black trail northwest passing a cattle guard (2.8, 265) and turn right onto a blue trail (4.2, 290). After about 200 meters make another left turn onto a green trail (4.4, 320). The green trail winds southeast and arrives at an observation point facing Mt. Tabor (5.7, 260). Pass under a power line (7.1, 330) and arrive at a trail junction (7.2, 340).

Take the INT south and climb Mt. Debora. The INT makes a right turn onto a fine dirt road black trail (8.3, 380). At the top of Mt. Debora take a break (9.1, 435). *There is an excellent view of Mt. Tabor from the east side of Mt. Debora. And you will find here a memorial in honor of the 25th wedding anniversary of Queen Elizabeth II and her husband Prince Philip.* From the top take the blue trail down and north. Arrive at a road and a trail junction: black and red (10.0, 300).

From this point the hike is on a non marked trail.

Turn left on a paved road. Continue on a mild ascent, passing a beautiful vista (12.2, 350) and a picnic area (13.7, 365). Arrive at Nazareth Illit and turn left at a T junction (14.8, 380). Turn left on Havradim Street (15.0, 370). You will see a lawn on your right. Turn left on a dirt road (15.1, 365). Hike west through a forest of pine trees on a mild descent. The village of Iksal is visible below (16.7, 300). Arrive at a fork and continue down the left dirt road (17.0, 285). Pass a fence and a small structure on your right (17.1, 280). Turn left on a moderate ascent and after a sharp turn right pass by a large concrete water reservoir and a paved road (17.3, 270). Hike west and the paved road turns left. Do not continue left on the paved road but follow a dirt road straight ahead. Continue the descent and pass the houses of Iksal. Turn right at the lowest point of the descent (18.0, 240) and climb a dirt road, passing an old ruined house (18.4, 270). Continue down and turn left at a barbed-wire fence (18.6, 225). Continue down and turn right and west (18.9, 205). Pass cypress trees on your left and a barn on your right (19.4, 190).

Turn right and begin a moderate ascent on a dirt road toward Mt. Precipice (20.6, 160). The ascent arrives just above the west entrance to the tunnel on route 60 (21.0, 180). Make a sharp turn right on a white dirt road. After about 100 meters turn left onto a trail and begin the final ascent to Mt. Precipice (21.2, 190). *The ascent to Mt. Precipice is part of the Gospel Trail.* The trail veers on a steep ascent. As you go up you will see the unfolding vista of Mt. Tabor and the beautiful Jezreel valley. There is a metal handrail (21.3, 240) and a security metal cable (21.5, 280). The steep ascent ends above the tunnel entrance, providing a beautiful view to the south (21.8, 360). The trail turns north and continues on a mild ascent among pine trees. Arrive at a parking lot and the summit of Mount Precipice (22.4, 400). Take another look at Mt. Tabor and the Jezreel valley from the observation point. Call a taxi to take you to downtown Nazareth, a 10 minute ride. Tel: 04-6462626, 04-6000164, 04-6081000 or 04-6555536. Mt. Precipice in Hebrew is Har Hakfitza.

From Nazareth to Jerusalem

You can continue the pilgrimage on the Israel National Trail and arrive after about two weeks and 265 kilometers in the Holy City of Jerusalem.

When you climb **Mount Carmel** and arrive to Isfiya visit the nearby Carmelites monastery which stands at the traditional site where Elijah confronted 450 Baal prophets: *1 Kings 18:21 : Elijah went before the people and said, "How long will you waver between two opinions? If the LORD is God, follow him; but if Baal is God, follow him."*

From Isfiya it's only a short ride by bus to **Haifa** and the **Bahá'í World Center**. Three days later you will hike on the Mediterranean shore at the gates of the magnificent ancient city of **Caesarea Maritima**. It was built by Herod the Great at about 25-13 BCE. **Apostle Paul** pleaded his case in Caesarea to be released from charges of inciting a riot in Jerusalem, with his preaching of the gospel. Further south pass ancient Arsuf (Phoenician name) or **Apollonia** (Hellenistic name), where the crusaders created the Lordship of Arsur 1101-1187 CE, as part of the Kingdom of Jerusalem. The vibrant city of **Tel Aviv** is the next stop on the trail. **Ancient Jaffa** is a must visit when in Tel Aviv.

From Tel Aviv you will continue the hike and after three days you will climb for two more days the Judean Mountains and arrive to **Jerusalem**.

For the Israel National Trail guide that includes all the topographical maps (1:50,000) of the trail see in bibliography or visit:

http://www.i-sys.co.il/eng.html

Jerusalem

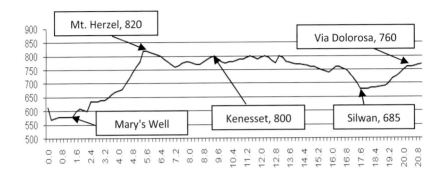

Hiking the Jerusalem Trail is a unique experience. The 20 kilometer hike will take you to historic and archaeological sites, you will meet fascinating people of all religions, and you will visit one of the most exciting cities in the world. You will complete the pilgrimage at the Holy Sepulchre. Since there are so many sites on or near the trail it is impossible to describe them all in detail, so I have decided to limit them to one or two lines. Please visit www.jerusalemp3.com to download free audio tours to your mp3 player. Visit the Jerusalem city website for information about attractions, free guided tours, accommodations and events. www.jerusalem.muni.il. For English click **ENG** at the top left corner.

The trail is clearly marked outside the city. Blue trail markers are clear and wooden posts are placed along the trail. Within the city some trail markers are visible when you hike in a clockwise direction but they are somewhat difficult to discern if you are going the other way. In the section between the Hebrew University on Mount Scopus (Har Hatzofim) and Giv'at Hatakhmoshet trail markers are sparse, and the trail has not yet been marked from Giv'at Hatakhmoshet to the Chords Bridge at the exit to the city. This section is not included in the guide.

We have divided the Jerusalem hike into two days for purposes of description, but we recommend to extend the hike and take the time to visit the many interesting sites along the way in the city of Jerusalem.

Day 13: Ein Karem to Emek Refaim Street - 15 km

Maps: 13-17. You can buy water all along the trail from the entrance to Ein Karem.

If you hiked from Nazareth to Jerusalem on the Israel National Trail, you will continue to Ein Karem from Ein Hindak at km 0.2 of the hike description, 200 meters from Even Sapir. If you came to Jerusalem by public transportation we recommend starting day 10 in Ein Karem, at km 3.3 of the day. You can spend the night at the Rosary Sisters Guesthouse in Ein Karem, next to the Church of the Visitation. See in accommodations.

To get to Even Sapir *take Egged bus number 27a from the central bus station on Yafo Street (06:25, and 09:50). Alternatively you can ride bus 27 that goes to Hadassah Medical Center every 15 minutes, and take a taxi to Even Sapir. It is a 3 minute ride (ask the driver to turn on the meter). You can also hike from Hadassah to Even Sapir, a 1.8 km hike on the road. From Hadassah go down on route 386 and turn left after about 100 meters.. Continue on the road until you reach Even Sapir.*

To get to Ein Karem *from the central bus station take Egged bus number 27 or 27a, and change at Mt. Herzl to bus number 28 or 28a (every 10-15 minutes). When you come to Ein Karem get off at the main street, turn left to Hama'ayan Street and turn right at Mary's well, by the Ein Karem Music Center. Pass the entrance to the Rosary Sisters Guesthouse and another 50 meters further you will come to the entrance road of the Visitation Church.*

St. John in the Desert Monastery is just 15 minutes walk in Even Sapir. Take the main road down to the monastery. The road makes a sharp turn to the right and 500 meters further on it makes a left turn down. Arrive at the monastery after another 700 meters. Remains of a 6th century monastery were found here. The place was rebuilt by the Crusaders. The present monastery was built in 1922. Open: Sun-Fri 08:00-12:00 14:00-17:00. Sat: 08:00-17:00. Allow 30 minutes for the visit.

Start the 150 meters from the entrance to Even Sapir (615, 0.0). A steep descent down a short trail will bring you to Ein Hindak (570, 0.2). At the fork in the path take the blue trail right and north, it is the Jerusalem trail.

The green trail is the Israel National Trail, do not take it. Outside of Jerusalem the trail is indicated with blue trail markers. The symbol of Jerusalem - a blue and gold sign with the emblem of a lion – accompanies you within the city and sometimes outside as well. In built up areas the city trail is indicated by blue and gold markers. Follow the dirt track. This was the ancient Roman road leading from Ein Hindak. You will see a road that joins up on the right, from the direction of the Hadassah hospital (0.6, 580). As you continue walking and pass through an old gate, the path climbs gently and then descends slightly. On your left you will see a building above a spring, and some 200 meters further, a small building over another spring above you to your right. The path climbs moderately to the right and becomes a pedestrian path (1.5, 580). It continues to climb and then levels out. Before you get to route 396 there are steps to climb. Climb over the security railing and take care as you cross the road. On the other side is a gate and a signpost pointing to Hadassah and Jerusalem (1.7, 600). The red-green markers of the Hadassah trail can sometimes be seen on signs placed in the ground.

Keep walking north on the dirt track as it curves east. Turn right at the fork, following the moderate upward gradient. A further gentle climb brings you to another fork (2.1, 610) where you will find a trail sign for those ascending to Ein Kerem and for those descending to Ein Hindak, and a sign for the Hadassah trail. Keep going east at the fork. Hadassah medical center is now clearly visible above you. You will pass a picnic area, a high voltage pylon, and a Hadassah trail sign (point no. 13). Stop here to enjoy the magnificent vista (2.5, 600), then continue straight before turning right for a steep but short climb. Follow the path as it veers left between olive trees and Jerusalem pines. You will cross an avenue of cypresses. Between the trees on your right you can see a wooden sign indicating the entrance to the Hadassah trail (2.9, 635). Keep going east. A steep but very short climb on a concrete road leads to a dirt path. Continue east and arrive to the entrance way of the *Church of the Visitation* (3.3, 630). Turn right and after a short climb by steps arrive at the gate of the Church.

Luke 1:39-40: "Now Mary arose in those days and went into the hill country with haste, to a city of Judah, and entered the house of Zacharias and greeted Elizabeth." This event is the "Visitation" commemorated by the present church, which is reputed to stand on the site where the event took place.

The Church of the Visitation incorporates a natural grotto that once contained a small spring. The grotto was a place of worship in the Byzantine period, and the Crusaders erected a large, two-storey church over it. The church collapsed after the Crusaders left. In 1679 the site was bought by the Franciscans. Two centuries later they received permission from the Ottoman authorities to restore the church. The lower section was restored in 1862 and the upper church was completed in 1955, according to plans drawn up by Antonio Barluzzi.

Luke 1:46-49: "My soul magnifies the Lord, and my spirit has rejoiced in God my Savior. For He has regarded the lowly state of His maidservant; For behold, henceforth all generations will call me blessed; For He who is mighty has done great things for me and holy is His name".

One wall of the church courtyard is covered with ceramic tiles bearing the words of the Magnificat in more than 40 languages. Open: Apr.-Sept. 08:00-12:00; 14:30-18:00; Oct.-Mar. 08:00-12:00; 14:30:17:00. Gates are closed on Saturdays. Ring the bell to be admitted.

Return to the trail after the visit. Passing the boundary wall of the convent of the Rosary Sisters (3.35, 640) you will have a nice view of Ein Kerem. At Mary's Well (3.5, 640) turn left onto Hama'ayan Street and left again on Ein Kerem Street (3.8, 635), climbing gradually until you reach Kastel Square (4.0, 650). A blue and gold marker can be seen on the wall on the left side of Ein Kerem Street, opposite the parking lot.

Cross to the other side of Ein Kerem Street, go up Hatzelafim Street (medium gradient), and pass the Church of St. John the Baptist. Keep going east on Shvil Hatzukim Street until you come to a dirt road (4.8, 670) where you will see another blue marker. Keep going west, climbing gradually. Pass an entrance (5.1, 680) and continue east on the Shvil Hatzukim dirt road. The path veers to the left and climbs steeply through a grove. Go up the wooden stairs until you reach Hazichron Street, the road leading left and west towards **Yad Vashem Holocaust Memorial Center. Open: Sun-Wed 09:00-17:00; Thu: 09:00-20:00; Fri: 09:00-14:00. Sat and holidays closed. Last entry is admitted one hour before the museum closes. Free.** Turn right and east and arrive at Holland Square and Herzl Street (6.3, 820). Water and toilets are available at the entrance to Mt. Herzl. Turn left on Herzl Street and walk down the road to Bet Yad Sarah. Keep going straight and note the trail markers on the fence outside buildings 109 and 118. When you reach Kikar Denya (Denmark Square) (8.1, 760) turn right and cross Herzl Boulevard in the direction of Ariel Tamas Street (you will see a marker on the steps). After passing the monument to the fallen fighters of the Bet Hakerem neighborhood you will come to Hechalutz Street. Turn right at the Bet Hakerem council building and after 20 meters turn left into Haviva Reich Street. Continue straight on Hagai Street until you come to a public park (9.1, 760). Go through the park and walk across the pedestrian bridge straddling the Begin Expressway. Turn left at the end of the bridge, pass the Jerusalem Academy High School for Music and Dance and continue in the direction of the Givat Ram parking lot (toilets are available). Turn right and immediately left to the exit road from Givat Ram.

You will now come to Kaplan Street, opposite the Bank of Israel and Kiryat Hamemshala (the government complex) (9.7, 780). Turn right and continue on Ruppin Street until you reach the *Israel Museum intersection (9.5, 770). The museum is open: Sun, Mon, Wed, Thu, Sat 10:00-17:00; Tue 16:00-21:00; Fri: 10:00-14:00.* Turn left on Kaplan Street, go up to the Knesset area, and turn right at the first intersection. Follow the path as it curves left into the Rose Garden (9.9, 790). Take the time to visit the Menora located 50 meters above the road. From this vantage point you have an excellent view of the Knesset. (Some 20 meters further there are public facilities). Go back to the entrance of the Rose Garden, climb the steps and turn right on the asphalt path winding to the left. From this vantage point you can see both the Knesset and the Supreme Court. The layout is no accident, it was deliberately planned to symbolize the close connection between parliament and the court of justice. Keep going in the direction of the Supreme Court and then turn right and go back in the direction of the Knesset (toilets are available on your left, next to the fence of the Supreme Court). After descending approximately 100 meters turn right. The Knesset guards' station is located some 50 meters further (10.3, 800). Turn left and walk downhill in the direction of the bird watching station of the Society for the Protection of Nature in Israel. Here you will find a bird feeding station where wintering birds are ringed.

Continue walking down the hill, turn left in the direction of Sacher Park, and then right. Keep going straight until you reach the tunnel under Ruppin Street (11.0, 775). Cross at the tunnel and continue and turning left at another tunnel beneath Haim Hazaz Street (11.2, 770).

The Valley of the Cross is on your right. Continue straight down, turn right and you will arrive at the monastery. The Monastery of the Cross is a Byzantine structure. It derives its name from the tradition that the olive tree used to make Christ's cross grew at this site. The monastery was built in the 11th century over the remains of a 4th century monastery. Mon-Sat: 10:00-17:00 (fee).

Go back to the tunnel cross it and at the exit turn right to the sidewalk and after 20 meters turn sharply right. Another 200 meters will bring you to a beautiful view of the Valley of the Cross on your right. Now go up to your right until you reach Sa'adia Gaon Street and at the intersection with Metudela Street continue left on Sa'adia Gaon Street. The street name changes to Alfasi Street. Look for building no. 25. Prime Minister Menachem Begin and his wife Aliza lived here in the 1940s, in the basement apartment with green shades which is at the bottom of the path leading to the house. Continue on Alfasi Street. Some 100 meters further you will see on your left the tomb of Jason, a High Priest in the time of the Second Temple, during the Hellenist (Greek) period (800, 12.3). Turn right and continue on Radak Street, cross Aza Street and keep walking until you reach a parking lot, then turn right and walk up the road to the President's Residence (800, 13.0). Turn left at Shneourson Street and after 100 meters turn left again onto Chopin Street.

On your right on Palmach Street is the Islamic Art museum, where you will find the famous David Lionel Salomons collection of Breguet watches. The pride of the collection is the watch designed for Marie Antoinette, who commissioned a timepiece that would incorporate every watch function known at that time. She never lived to see the watch, as it was only completed 34 years after her execution. In 1983 the famous watch collection was stolen by Na'aman Diller. After his death, some 25 years later, the watches were found and restored to the museum. The museum is open on Sun, Mon, Wed.

10:00-15:00; Tue, Thu 10:00-19:00; Fri 10:00-14:00 Sat 10:00-16:00.
http://www.islamicart.co.il/en/

Continue Passing the Jerusalem Theater and continuing straight to Dubnow Street. When you come to a grove of pines – Gan Lior – continue to your right (there are no markers) onto a dirt path. Follow the path as it descends to Gedalia Alon Street, near the Hartman Institute. Turn left and continue to Dor Dor Vedorshav Street, where you will see a brown sign indicating that you have reached the Nature Museum. Water and toilets are available there.

Continue to Graetz Street (14.1, 760) and turn right. Turn left at Emek Refaim Street. Keep walking until you reach Mendes France Square (14.7, 760) by the gas station (water and toilets). Cross at the intersection and arrive at the gate of the Scottish Church and Hotel.

Day 14: Emek Refaim Street to the Holy Sepulchre - 6 km

Maps: 17-18. You can buy water along the trail.

Start at the gate of the Scottish Church Hotel (0.0, 760). Go down S.A. Nachon Street, pass by the **Menahem Begin Heritage Center**. *Open Sun, Mon, Wed, Thu 09:00-16:30; Tue: 09:00-19:00; Fri 09:00-12:30; Sat: Closed.* Continue down and cross the B'nai B'rith Bridge that spans Hebron Road (0.5, 740).

Bethlehem and the Church of the Nativity *is just 8 kilometers to the south. To get to Bethlehem turn right and go up Hebron Road. Continue south and after about 4.5 kilometers you will cross the border to the Palestinian Authority. After 3.5 km you will arrive at Bethlehem. Check visa requirements at your consulate, a travel agency, or your hotel.*

To visit the ***Room of the Last Supper*** do not turn right on the blue trail but continue down Hebron Road. Cross the bridge and turn right at the stop light (0.75, 730) on Hativat Yerushalaim Street. Turn left at a small parking lot (1.0, 750) and after 50 meters turn right into a narrow alley. Turn left through a gate (1.2, 760) to the traditional site of King's David Tomb. The Room of the Last Supper is located above King David's Tomb. Exit to an alley and you will see a set of stairs leading to the Room of the Last Supper (1.35, 760)

Mark 14:15-17 "And he will show you a large upper room furnished and ready; there prepare for us." And the disciples set out and went to the city and found it just as he had told them, and they prepared the Passover. And when it was evening, he came with the twelve". Open: Sat-Thu 08:00-17:00; Fri 08:00-13:00; Sun: Closed, free. Allow 15 minutes.

Opposite the Room of the Last Supper is the **The Dormition of the Virgin Mary Abbey - Hagia Maria Sion**. *It was on this spot, near the Room of the Last Supper, that Mary died. The Basilica was built over the remains of a Byzantine church and was dedicated in 1910.* Open: Mon, Tue, Wed, Fri 8:30-12:00 and 12:30-18:00; Thu. 9:45-12:00 and 12:30-17:30; Sat. 8:30-12:00 and 12:30-17:30; Sun 10:30-11:45 and 12:30-17:30. Allow 30 minutes.

Retrace your steps through King David's Tomb and when you arrive back to the parking lot (1.7, 750) cross the street, turn right and go down. After a very short distance turn left and go toward Gey Ben Hinnom Street. At Ben Hinnom Street turn left and after another 300 meters you will have rejoined the trail (2.4, 700). The road drops at a steep gradient to the village of Silwan (2.6, 680). Turn left at the brown sign that points the way to Ir David (David's City). Continue another 300 meters along Hashiloach Street and after the road turns left (3.5, 685) a steep climb (to the left) will bring you to Ir David. If you want to continue on to the Old City and the Kotel you should turn left at the rise.

Walk through the village along Hashiloach Street until the paved road turns into a dirt road (3.9, 690). Markers can be seen on the electricity poles. The road climbs moderately until you enter the area of Har Hazeitim (Mt. of Olives) cemetery. The walls of the Old City tower over you on your left. Turn right, and you will see the grave of Zekharya ben Yehoyada, with the grave of Absalom immediately beyond (4.2, 700). Climb the steps towards Jericho Road. There are public toilets on the way. When you reach Jericho Road (4.4, 720) the Russian Church of Mary Magdalene with its gleaming golden onion-shaped domes will be on your right while the Old City is on your left. Turn left on Jericho road and follow the path in front of the Church of all Nations which stands next to the garden of Gethsemane (4.5, 730).

Matthew 26:36: Then Jesus went with his disciples to a place called **Gethsemane**, *and he said to them, "Sit here while I go over there and pray."*

To enter **Gethsemane** turn right on El-Manssuria Street. After a very short ascent turn right (4.7, 735). Ancient olive trees grow in the garden. The Church of All Nations stands on the remains of a Byzantine church that was destroyed by an earthquake in the 8th century, and a 12th century Crusader church which was abandoned in the 14th century. Open daily Oct-Mar: 08:00-12:00 and 14:00-17:00; Apr-Sep: 08:00-12:00 and 14:00-18:00.

From Mt. Olives there is a spectacular view of the Old City. From Gethsemane turn right and immediately make another right turn. Climb the narrow and steep street until you've reached an observation point. The Russian Orthodox Church of Mary Magdalene is on your way. Open Tuesdays and Thursdays 10:00-12:00.

The Jerusalem trail goes right and up when you Leave Gethsemane. You turn left and down (there are public restrooms across the street, small fee). Turn right on Jericho road off the Jerusalem trail (there are no trail markers from this point) and go down to the **Tomb of the Virgin Mary**. Steps from the road descend into a square courtyard containing the upper church, which is a Crusader church with a vault for the family of King Baldwin the 2nd. The lower church at the bottom of the stairs is a Byzantine (5th century) **crypt.** There is an apse to the west and a longer, rock-cut apse to the east, in which **Mary's tomb** is marked by a small square chapel. Open daily: Mon-Sat 08:00-12:00 and 14:00-17:00.

Return to Jericho Road, turn right, make an immediate left turn and after a short climb you will come to the entrance to the Old City at the Lion's Gate (5.2, 760). Enter the Old City. For many Christian pilgrims to Jerusalem, their most important and meaningful experience is the walk along the **Via Dolorosa**, following the route taken by Jesus after his condemnation by Pilate, on his way to his crucifixion and burial. The Via Dolorosa has evolved since the 4th century un early Christianity, but for most pilgrims, the exact location of each event along the Via Dolorosa is of minor importance; the significance of the pilgrimage lies in its proximity to the original events and the opportunity to reflect upon them along the way. Stations are marked with a small plaque and are not easy to spot.

Below is the list of the stations along the Via Dolorosa:

Station 1: Where Jesus was condemned by Pontius Pilate. Today it is **the School of Madrasa al-Omariya,** 300m west of the Lion's Gate Open: Mon-Thu, Sat, 14:30-18:00; Fri 14:30-16:00.

Station 2: Where Jesus took up his cross. It is across the road from the first Station, in the Franciscan Monastery of the Flagellation,

Station 3: Where Jesus fell for the first time under the weight of his cross. It is marked by a relief sculpture above the door of a small Polish chapel at the junction with al-Wad Road.

Station 4: Where Mary watched her son pass by bearing the cross. It is commemorated at the Armenian Church of Our Lady of the Spasm. Inside the church is a Byzantine floor mosaic.

Station 5: Where Simon of Cyrene was forced by Roman soldiers to help Jesus carry the cross. It is located on the corner where the Via Dolorosa turns west off al-Wad Road and begins to narrow as it goes uphill.

Station 6 is commemorated by the **Greek Catholic Church of the Holy Face**.

Station 7: Where Jesus fell for a second time. It is marked by a Franciscan chapel at the junction of the Via Dolorosa and Souq Khan al-Zeit.

Station 8: Where Jesus consoled the lamenting women of Jerusalem. It is across the market street and up the steps of Aqabat al-Khanqah, opposite the Station VIII Souvenir Bazaar. A cross and the Greek inscription NIKA can be seen on the wall of the Greek Orthodox **Monastery of St. Charalambos**.

Station 9 is at the Coptic Patriarchate next to the Church of the Holy Sepulchre. Here, a Roman pillar marks the site of Jesus' third fall.

The remaining stations are inside The Church of the Holy Sepulchre (5.7, 800).

Station 10: Jesus is stripped - top of the stairs to the right outside the entrance.

Station 11: Jesus is nailed to the Cross, upstairs inside the entrance, at the Latin Calvary.

Station 12: Jesus dies on the Cross. Rock of Golgotha in the Greek Orthodox Calvary.

Station 13: Jesus is taken down from the Cross. Statue of Our Lady of the Sorrows – Latin Calvary.

Station 14: Jesus is laid in the Tomb, is inside the tiny chapel of the Holy Sepulchre.

The Church of the Holy Sepulchre, (6.0, 760) known as the Church of the Resurrection (*Anastasis*) to Eastern Orthodox Christians, is the holiest Christian site in the world. It stands on a site that is believed to encompass both Golgotha, or Calvary, where Jesus was crucified, and the tomb (sepulchre) where he was buried. The Church of the Holy Sepulchre has been an important destination for pilgrims since the 4th century. The construction of the Holy Sepulchre was begun in 324 CE, under Emperor **Constantine the Great,** who converted to Christianity. It was destroyed by fire in 614 CE and rebuilt in 630 CE. Following a period of Moslem rule Emperor **Constantine Monomachos** provided money for its reconstruction in 1048. In later centuries it was damaged, and the Franciscans undertook its restoration in 1550. The structure was severely damaged by a fire in 1808 and an earthquake in 1927. Only in 1960 did major communities agreed on a plan of renovation. Open daily: Apr-Sep 05:00-20:00; Oct-Mar: 05:00-19:00.

Major sites in the Old City

The Western Wall and Temple Mount are within a short walking distance of the Church of the Holy Sepulchre.

The Western Wall - (The Kotel) : Open 24 hours. Make sure to visit Western Wall tunnels. Open: Sun-Thu 07:00-18:00. Fri: 07:00-12:00. Guided tours only in Hebrew, English and French. (Fee).

Temple Mount: The Dome of the Rock and Al-Aksa Mosque.   Summer: Mon-Thu 07:30-10:30; 13:30-14:30. Winter: Mon-Thu 07:30-10:30; 12:30-13:30. The mosques are closed to tourists.

Accommodations

Accommodations are listed from Nazareth to the Sea of Galilee and back to Nazareth, according to the hike description. The following accommodations are listed below: Trail angels, private and free camping sites, hostels and other budget accommodation, B&B and hotels. Contact information is provided for all types of accommodation where available. Many places have free internet access. Inquire upon reservation.

Trail angels and low cost accommodations

There are a few trail angels along the trail. The list of trail angels is continuously updated on the web. The list also includes low cost accommodations along the trail. Trail angels are listed from north to south. Go to:

http://shvil.wikia.com/wiki/INT_Trail_Angels

Camping

Day 2: Lavi forest camping, free. Water and picnic tables. Restrooms are open 07:00-16:00. Located east of the Golani junction. From the gas station (day 2 km 12.0) do not cross route 77 but hike east on a dirt road and after approximately 500 meters you will arrive at a road that leads right and south to the camping site.

Sea of Galilee camping

Camping sites on the shores of the Sea of Galilee can be very crowded in spring and summer, especially on weekends and holidays.

Tamar beach camping. NIS 50. Shower, restrooms, restaurant. Cabins are available. Hike north from Migdal along route 90 for about 400 meters. Turn right on a road that arrives at the camp site after another 600 meters. Tel: 04-6790630; 050-5852101.

Hukok beach camping. NIS 50. Shower, restrooms, grocery store. From the Hukok junction (route 8077 and route 90) hike north on the trail along route 90 and after about 500 meters cross route 90 and hike east on a road that arrives at the camp site after about 1 km. Karei Deshe IYHA hostel is also located on the Hukok beach. *An 8ᵗʰ century palace and a mosaic were found at nearby Hirbat Manim.* Tel: 04-6715440.

Day 7: Kinneret beach camping: NIS 40. Shower, restrooms, restaurant. Tel: 04-6759499.

Day 7: Yavne'el camping: Camping NIS 50-70; Cabins NIS 100. Shower and restrooms. Grocery store within walking distance. Cell: 050-5277345 (Neri); Tel: 04-6708770; Fax: 04-6708045. Across route 767 when you exit Nahal Yavne'el or 1 km north of the exit from the village on route 767 at Tel Yin'am. Pickup available from the trail (Fee).

Day 7 (8) : Ein Ulam. Free. Camp on the trail at Ein Ulam, There are no facilities and no water. Located at km 9.9 of day 8, 18 kilometers from Yardenit. **Fill up 6-7 liters of water in Yardenit**, next refill is in Kfar Kish.

Day 10 (9): Shibli camping. NIS 55. Shower, restrooms. Grocery store within walking distance. Coffee or tea provided free of charge. Located in Shibli, 2 kilometers west of the entrance to the village from the Gazit junction. After the descent from Mt. Tabor turn right and the camping is on your left. Tel: 052-3106103 Sami.

Hostels and Inns

Sleep in dormitories or private rooms where available. Low rate indicates dormitories single occupancy, high rate is for private room double occupancy unless otherwise specified.

ILH - Israel Hostels: Nazareth, Tiberias, Kfar Tavor, Haifa, Tel-Aviv and Jerusalem are the ILH hostels close to the trail and in major cities. ILH offers a wide choice of accommodations at competitive prices. Book on-line at: www.hostels-israel.com

Israel Youth Hostels Association (IYHA): IYHA provides a discount of 5% to guests presenting this guide at check-in. Double discounts are not available. Reservations are recommended. National reservation line: Tel: 1-599-510-511 press 4 for English, or book on-line at:

http://www.iyha.org.il/eng. Poriya & Karei Deshe (near the Sea of Galilee – Kinneret – area), Tel Aviv, Jaffa and Jerusalem are the IYHA hostels closest to the trail or in major cities.

Nazareth

- *Fauzi-Azar Inn.* NIS 90 dormitories / NIS 440-500 double in a private room. Rates include breakfast. Located in the heart of Nazareth, just 5 minutes walk from the Church of the Annunciation. Tel: 04-6020469; 054-4322328; www.fauziazarinn.com
- *Rosary Sisters Guest House.* Directions on their web site: http://rosarysisters.com/. Cell: 054-5533861.
- *Al-Mutran Guest House*: NIS 500 double. www.al-mutran.com Tel: 04-6457947; 052-7229090.
- *Sisters of Nazareth – Convent.* NIS 70 / 175-275. Tel: 04-6554304.
- *St. Margaret Hostel – Convent.* NIS 140 / 425. Tel: 04-657-3507.

Cana

Cana Guest House. NIS 100 / 300. Tel: 04-6517186; 04-6412375; Fax: 04-6518013. www.canaguesthouse.com. Contact them for directions.

Arbel

Shavit Hostel. NIS 120, B&B also available. NIS 550-800 double in private room. Tel: 04-6794919. E-mail: sara52@012.net.il .

Ginosar

Karei Deshe: IYHA hostel – NIS 450 B&B double. Located on the northeastern shore of the Sea of Galilee: E-mail: kdeshe@iyha.org.il ; Tel: 1-599-510511; 02-5945632. For directions see Hukok Beach camping.

Tiberias

Tiberias youth hostel: NIS 80-90 / 375. Tel: 04-679-2611; Fax: 04-6792411; www.tiberiashostel.com .
Aviv youth hostel: NIS 75 / 275-325. Tel: 04-6712272   http://ilh.hostels-israel.com/hotel-aviv/hostel

Poriya

Poriya IYHA Hostel: NIS 480 Tel: 1-599-510511; 02-5945577; E-mail: poria@iyha.org.il. Closed for renovations until September 2011.

Kfar Kish

Land of Galilee, family stay. NIS 150 single, www.landofgalilee.com Tel: 052-8606311.

Kfar Tavor

Hooha: B&B and hostel: NIS 150 / 480. Max. capacity 24. Tel/Fax: 077-8070524; Cell: 054-8070528; www.hooha.co.il/english_site.htm

B&B and family stay

B&B rates range between NIS 450-700 for double occupancy. Range indicates price on weekdays - weekends or holidays. All prices are in NIS (New Israeli Shekels) unless otherwise specified, and they are subject to change. Inquire if discount for Jesus trail hikers is available.

Zippori

Zippori village cottages B&B. Tel: 04-6462647; 057-7829568; E-mail: mspilcer@012.net.il
Zippori B&B: Tel: 04-6453373; 050-3100343.

Illaniya

Yehoshua B&B. Up to 8 people. Tel.: 054-4545210. For pickup and drop-off inquire when contacting the owner. E-mail: yehoshua18@walla.com.
Illaniya B&B. Up to 8 people. Pickup and drop-off available. Tel: 054-3137772; 04-676-9878.

Kfar Zeitim

Kfar Zeitim B&B. Up to 16 guests. Tel: 04-6796629; 052-3493546.

Arbel

Arbel B&B. Up to 40 guests. E-mail: arbelit@gmail.com. Tel: 04-6794325; 050-5700708.

Migdal

Beit Yehudit*: B&B.* Tel: 04-6724302; Cell: 052-2665238; Cell: 052-5208935 Max. capacity 16.

Weizman*: B&B.* Max. capacity 40. A 15% discount is provided to guests presenting this guide at check-in. Cell: 054-8015881; 0542400031; E-mail: yasmin_104@walla.co.il ;

Zohari*: B&B.* Tel: 04-67222304; Cell: 050-5502150; 050-6675087. Max. capacity 16.

Other B&Bs – There many B&Bs in Migdal, walk along the main street and look for one.

Tabgha

Mount of Beatitudes Hostel - Convent. $54 single B&B. Half / full board available. Send a fax for reservations. Tel: 04-672-6712; Fax: 04-6726735 E-mail: ospbeat@netvision.net.il ;

Vered Hagalil

B&B. NIS 550. Book on-line at: www.veredhagalil.com ; Tel: 04-6935785 ; Fax: 04-6934964 ; See advertisement.

Korazim

Beit Haerez B&B. www.bet-haerez.com/len/. Up to 25 guests. Tel: 04-6860990; 054-4000833.

Poriya

Poriya Illit B&B. Tel: 04-6751101; Cell: 050-8652517; E-mail: danybeery@gmail.com ; Up to 12 guests.

Yavne'el

B&B: Cell: 050-5305521; Tel: 04-6708672; E-mail: yhonatan@zahav.net.il; Pickup available from the trail.

B&B: E-mail: anettereuveni@gmail.com Cell: 052-8512983; 050-2512983

Hotels

Only hotels on the trail or within a short hiking distance from the trail are listed. For Nazareth hotels and other tourist information check: www.nazarethinfo.org/. For Tiberias hotels and other tourist information check: www.tiberis-hotels.com. Rates are B&B for double occupancy on weekdays.

- *Lavi Hotel:* NIS 700. E-mail: hotel@lavi.co.il; Tel: 04-6799450; Fax: 04-6799399. Discounts available for Jesus trail hikers. Kibbutz Lavi is a religious community, please do not call on Saturdays and Jewish holidays.
- *Ginosar Hotel:* NIS 550. Book on-line at: www.ginosar.co.il/en. Tel: 04-6700320; Fax: 04-6792170. Located in Ginosar off route 90. On day 4 from Migdal hike north on the rail and at the blue trail on km 8.7 turn right and east. Cross route 90 and continue towards the hotel on the entrance road to Ginosar.
- *Pilgerhause Tabgha:* NIS 700. Tel: 04-6700100 ; Fax: 04-6700101 ; E-mail: reception@tabgha.org.il ; Located at the entrance to Tabgha. When the trail arrives at Tabgha on route 87 turn right onto a road that goes south. It is a short walk of less than 500 meters.
- *Ohalo Manor hotel (Kinneret):* $110. Located about 1 km south of Kinneret (Moshava). On day 7 at km 6.2 (the Kinneret junction) turn right along route 90 and after approximately 1 km turn left toward the hotel. Book on-line at: http://www.ohalo.com/english. Tel: 04-6675526/7, reservations: 04-6675538 / 25.
- *Nof Tavor hotel – at Gazit junction:* NIS 450-500. On the trail at the Gazit junction (day 9 km 3.5). www.nof-tavor.com/?Lang=eng Tel: 04-6408000; Fax: 04-6408040.

Jerusalem

City of Jerusalem web site: http://tour.jerusalem.muni.il/eng

Ein Karem – the Rosary Sisters Guest House: NIS 300 (single room) – 800 (4 beds). In Ein Karem, on the trail next to the Church of the Visitation and the Music Center. www.rosary-einkarem.com. Tel: 02-6413755; Fax: 02-6419790.

Abraham Hostel: 67 Hanevi'im street, Tel: 02-6502200 E-mail: reservations@abrahamhostels.com; www.abrahamhostels.com.

IYHA: They have four locations in Jerusalem. http://www.iyha.org.il/eng/

Jerusalem Hostel: Tel: 02-6236102; Fax: 02-6236092; E-mail: reservation@jerusalem-hostel.com. www.jerusalem-hostel.com

Citadel Hostel: Tel: 02-6285253 E-mail: admin@citadelhostel.com.

Bibliography and additional reading

1. Israel National Trail and the Jerusalem Trail (English). Jacob Saar and Yagil Henkin. Eshkol 2011, ISBN: 978-965-91249-4-7.

2. Hiking the Jesus Trail. Anna Dintaman and Dave Landis. Village to Village Press 2010.

3. In the Footsteps of Jesus. W.E. Pax, Steimatzky and Nateev 1970.

4. Footsteps of Jesus. Hela Crown-Tamir, Gefen Publishing 2000.

5. The complete works of Josephus. Kregel Publications, MI USA, 1995.

6. Hiking in Israel. Yaacov Shkolnik and Yadin Roman, Toby Press 2008.

About the author

Jacob Saar (Ph.D.) has lived in Israel since 1957. He is a devoted hiker and has spent the last 40 years hiking the country. He has vast knowledge of the history of Israel. Jacob is the author of the Israel National Trail guide in both English and Hebrew. In addition to hiking the INT several times, he has hiked the Jesus Trail and every long trail in Israel.

Index

	Day		Day
Kfar Zeitim	4	Multiplication Church	6
Kibbutz Lavi	3	Nabi Shua'yb	4
King David Tomb	14	Nahal Amud	5
Kingdom of Jerusalem	4	Nahal Arbel	4
Kinneret	5, 8	Nahal Gazit	10
Kinneret	8	Nahal Nimerim	4
Kinneret (village)	9	Nahal Tavor	10
Knesset	13	Nahal Ulam	10
Korazim	7	Nahal Yavne'el	9
Last Supper Room	14	Natzeret Illit	1, 11, 12
Lazarists	5	Nazareth	1, 12
Lebanon	4	Nazareth Village	1
Livnim	5	Old Testament	1
Mary's Tomb	14	Ottoman	1, 5
Mary's well	1, 13	Peter's Primacy Church	6
Mashad	2, 11	Piacenza	1
Matthew	6	Pope John Paul II	6, 7
Mediterranean	3	Pope Paul VI	11
Menahamia	10	Poriya	8, 9
Menahem Begin	13, 14	Prince Philip	11
Mensa Christi	6	Queen Elizabeth	11
Mensa Christi Church	1, 2	Queen of Holland	3
Migdal	5, 7, 8	Reina	2
Mizpe	8	Roman road	3
Monastery of the Cross	13	Russian Church	14
Mount Arbel	4, 5, 8	Saladin	4
Mount Carmel	4	Salesian Sisters	2
Mount Debora	11, 12	Sea of Galilee	5, 6, 10
Mount Jona	11	Sheikh Tarif	4
Mount Nitai	4, 5	Shibli	11, 12
Mount of Beatitudes	6	Silwan	14
Mount of Olives	14	St. John in the desert	13
Mount Precipice	1, 11, 12	St. Peter	6
Mount Tabor	1, 11	Synagogue Church	1

	Day
Syria	1,4
Tabgha	5, 6
Talmud	1
Tel Rekesh	10
Templar	1
Temple Mount	14
The Holy Sepulcher	14
The Nativity Church	14
Tiberias	4, 8
Titus	5
Transfiguration Church	11
Tur'an	4
Tur'an valley	3
Twelve Apostles Church	6
Um Ranem	11
Valley of the Cross	13
Via Dolorosa	14
Via Maris	1, 6
Wailing wall	14
Wedding Church	2
White Mosque	1
Yad Vashem	13
Yardenit Baptismal site	9

Flowers of Israel

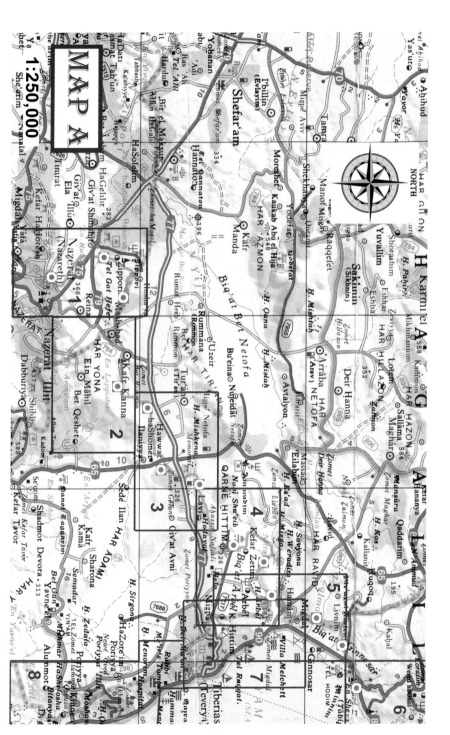

MAP A

1:250,000

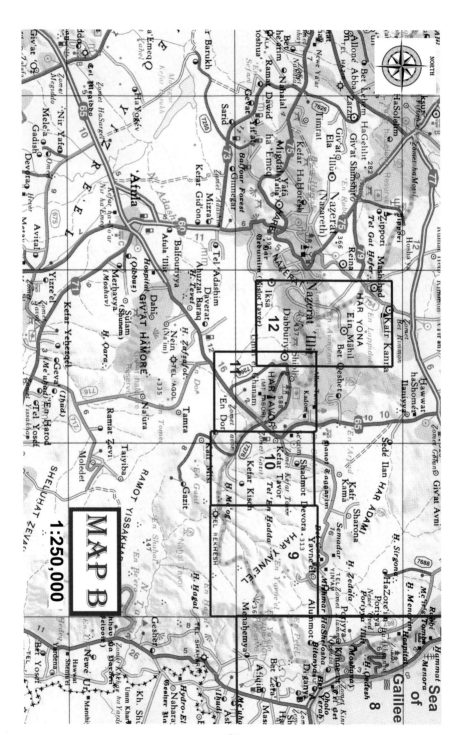

MAP B

1:250,000

Nazareth

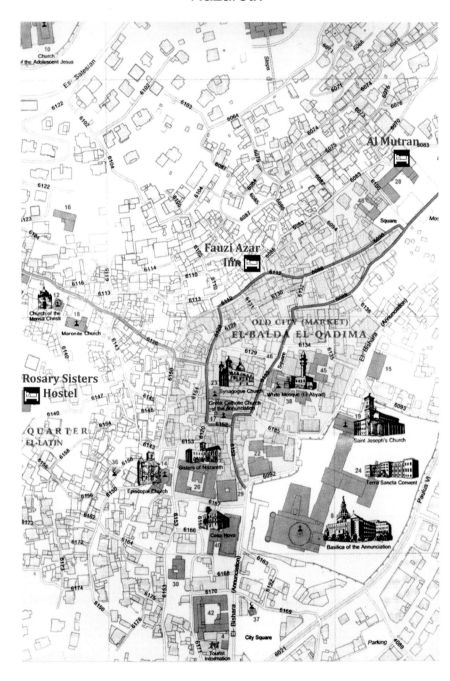

Legend

Scale 1:45,000

1000 Meters 500   0   1   2   3   4   Kilometers

1000 Yards 500   0   1   2   Miles

Symbol	Name	Symbol	Name	Symbol	Name
⊙	Tower	△ 304	Triangulation	▭	Artificial Pond, Pool
⚓	Lighthouse	. 327	Altitude (meters)		Pond, Lake
⚡	Radio transmission	큐 362	Reference altitude		Canal
ᴎᴌ	Archeological site	● ♪	Police station	●	Spring
◌ ◌	Low ground	● ♨	Pumping station		Well
○	Tree	✿	Water mill	○	Pit
⊤	Palm tree	∩	Cave		Tmeele (high underground water)
◌	Bush	◢◣	Quarry	○	Water reservoir
	Urban area	☁	———		Wall
◉	Hirba, Ruins				Unmarked border
?	Cemetery				Power line
▪	Building				Cliffs
♂	Synagogue				Steep slope
♠	Church, Monastery	— 100 — 90 —			Elevation (altitude) lines. 10 Meters each
♀♀	Mosque, Mosque & tower	Wadi River, brook			Wadi, River / brook
♦♀	Grave, Shiekh's grave	Ruins Intact			Aqueduct

Olive trees   Citrus trees   Orchards

Nature reserve National park   Woods   Vines

+ + + + + + + + + + + +
Blue line UN resolution 425 Israeli Lebanese border 2000   Swamp

Border marker + + + + + + ▲ + + + + + +		International border marked
— 50 — Station		Railroad + km stones
Underpass Bridge		Road class A
		Road class B
		Road / Avenue
		Paved road
B A		Unpaved road
		Jesus trail
		Israel National Trail
		Unmarked trail
● ◉		Israel National Trail with various markers
		Jerusalem Trail with markers
		Israel National Trail and crossing trails: Red, black, blue, green and unmarked trails

- ⊡ Jesus trail marker
- ⊡ Black trail marker
- ⊡ Blue trail marker

Jesus trail (orange dot) and a green trail

- ⊡ Green trail marker
- ⊡ Red trail marker

- ▣ Israel National Trail marker

Picture of INT marker

- ▥ Jerusalem Trail marker

Gospel Trail   **Gas Station**   **Picnic area**   ✝ **Church, basilica holy site**   🅷 **Hospital**

⛱ **Beach**   ▭ **Express way (/toll)**   ▭ **Major highway**   **B&B / Hotel**

⛺ **Camping**   ▭ **Regiomal highway**   ▭ **Secondary road**

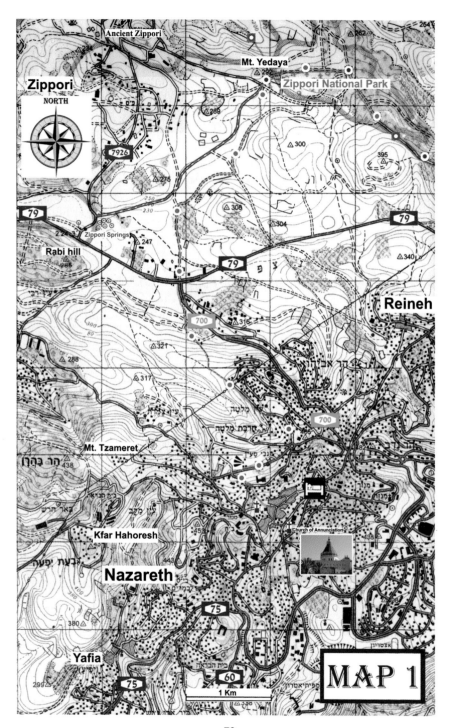

Zippori

NORTH

Ancient Zippori

Mt. Yedaya

Zippori National Park

79 26

Zippori Springs

Rabi hill

79

79

79

700

Reineh

Mt. Tzameret

Kfar Hahoresh

Church of Annunciation

Nazareth

75

Yafia

75

60

1 Km

MAP 1

Church of the Annunciation in Nazareth. Mona Lisa of the Galilee in Zippori

Moshav Arbel and the Arbel Valley. Mt. Arbel (right), Mt. Nitai (left)
and the Sea of Galilee

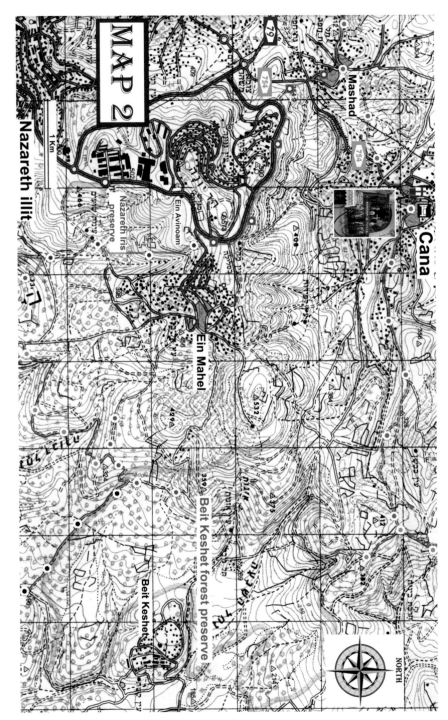

MAP 2

Nazareth illit

Nazareth

Nazareth Iris
preserve

Ein Avinoam

Ein Mahel

Beit Keshet forest preserve

Beit Keshet

Mashad

Cana

NORTH

1 Km

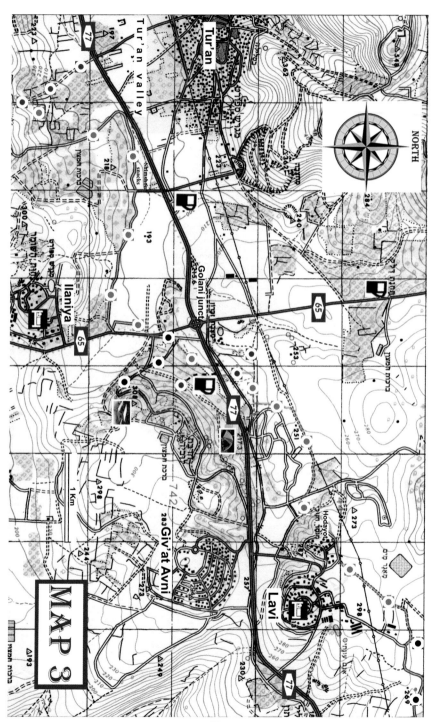

75

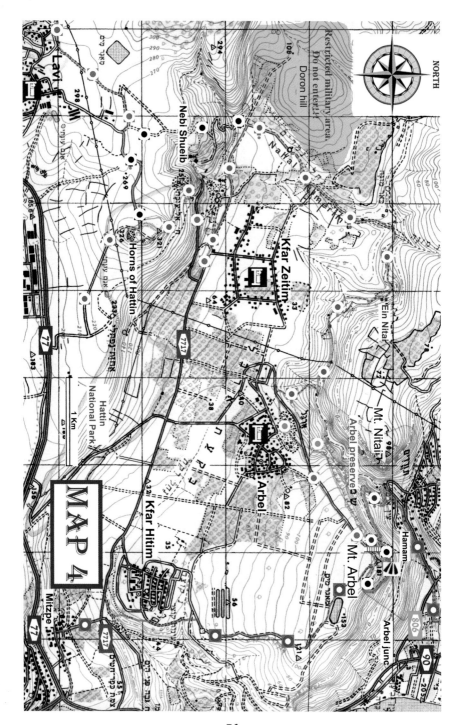

NORTH

Restricted military area.
Do not enter!!
Doron hill

294

106

Lavi

298

269

Nebi Shueib

Kfar Zeitim

Ein Nitai

Horns of Hattin

301

307

Mt. Nitain

96

Arbel preserve

Kfar Zeitim

31

7717

Hattin National Park

38

40

Arbel

82

Mt. Arbel

Hamam

MAP 4

Kfar Hitim

35

Mitzpe

77

7717

56

153

21

Arbel junc

805

90

1 Km

57

103

165.8

220

217

271

120

310

310

321

150

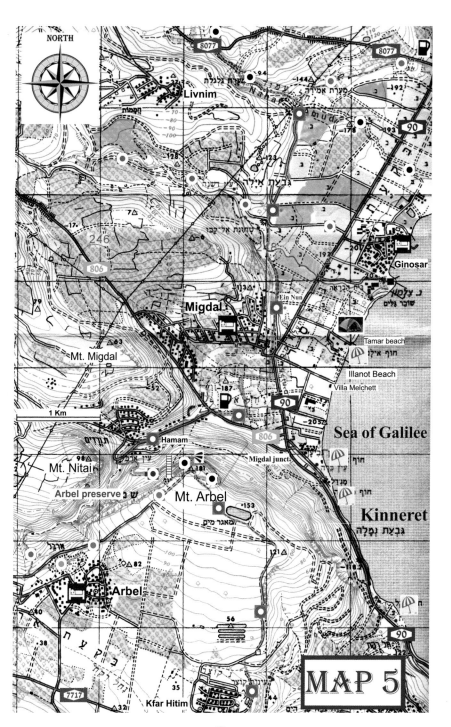

NORTH

8077
8077

מערת צלמת
94
144△
Nahal מערת אמירה
192
Livnim
176
193
90
128
123
גבעת אילי עין שנה
7△
246
806
13△
187
Ein Nun
207
Ginosar
Migdal
Tamar beach
חוף אילן
Illanot Beach
Villa Melchett
187
90
205
1 Km
806
Hamam
Sea of Galilee
Mt. Migdal
63
Migdal junct.
181
חוף
Mt. Nitai
Arbel preserve ש   Mt. Arbel
153
Kinneret
גבעת נפלה
82
121△
182
Arbel
56
90
40
38
122
7717
35
Kfar Hitim
32

MAP 5

77

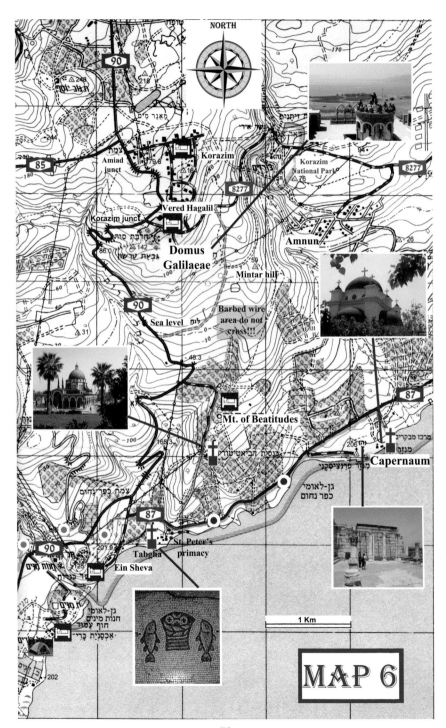

NORTH

MAP 6

Tabgha, Mt. Arbel (left), Horns of Hattin (middle distance), Mt. Nitai (right)

Mosaic of Loaves and Fishes in the Church of the Multiplication (left),
Fourth Century Synagogue, Capernaum

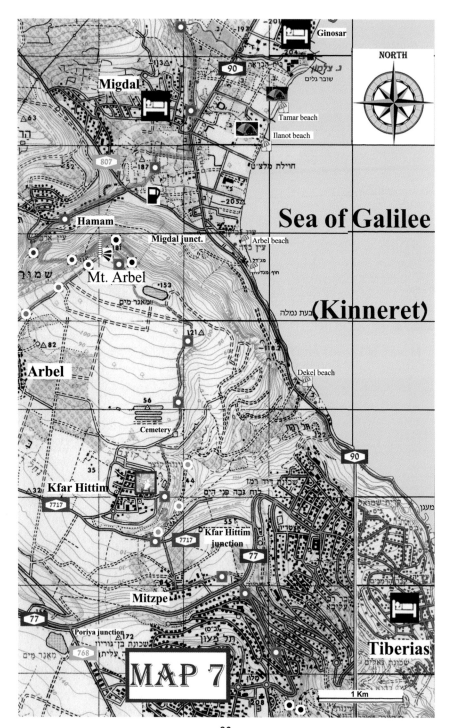

Ginosar

Migdal

Sea of Galilee

Hamam

Migdal junct.

Arbel beach

Mt. Arbel

(Kinneret)

Arbel

Dekel beach

Cemetery

Kfar Hittim

Kfar Hittim junction

Mitzpe

Poriya junction

Tiberias

MAP 7

1 Km

NORTH

Tamar beach

Ilanot beach

90

807

77

7717

768

77

90

80

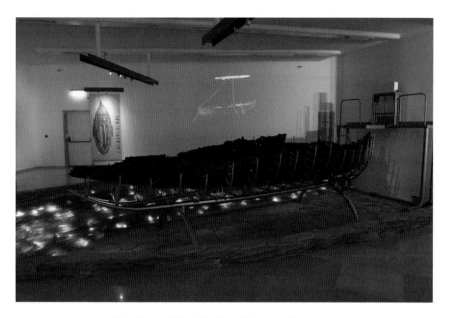

The Jesus Boat in the Ginosar Museum

Yardenit - Baptismal Site on the Jordan River

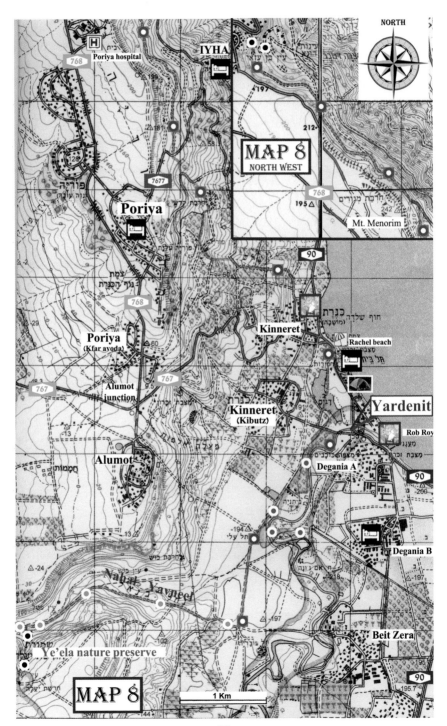

NORTH

Poriya hospital

IYHA

MAP 8
NORTH WEST

Mt. Menorim

Poriya

Poriya
(Kfar avoda)

Kinneret

Rachel beach

Alumot
junction

Kinneret
(Kibutz)

Yardenit

Rob Roy

Alumot

Degania A

Degania B

Nahal Yavneel

Ye'ela nature preserve

Beit Zera

MAP 8

1 Km

82

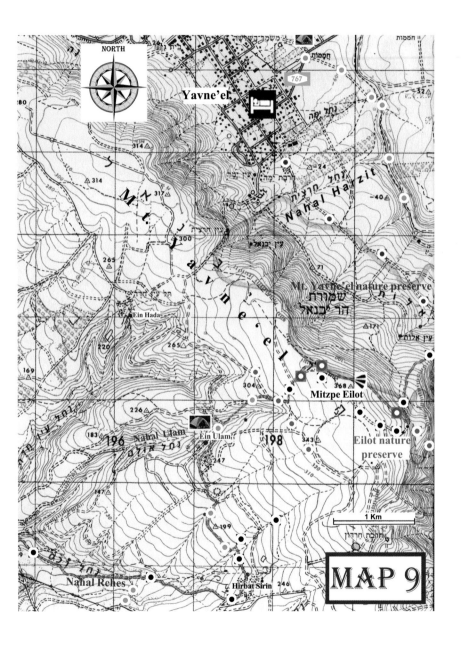

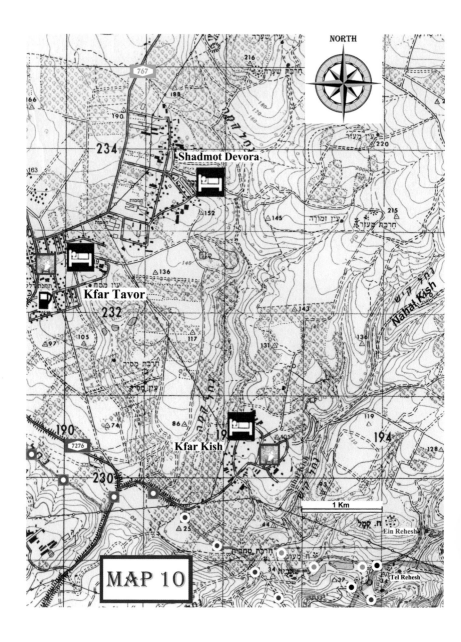

MAP 10

84

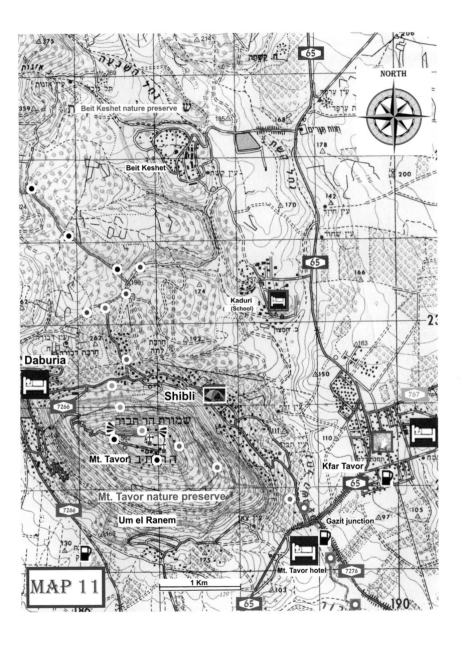

MAP 11

1 Km

85

Storks fly over the Yavne'el Valley
The Church of Transfiguration on Mt. Tabor
Pine forest at the foot of Mt. Devora

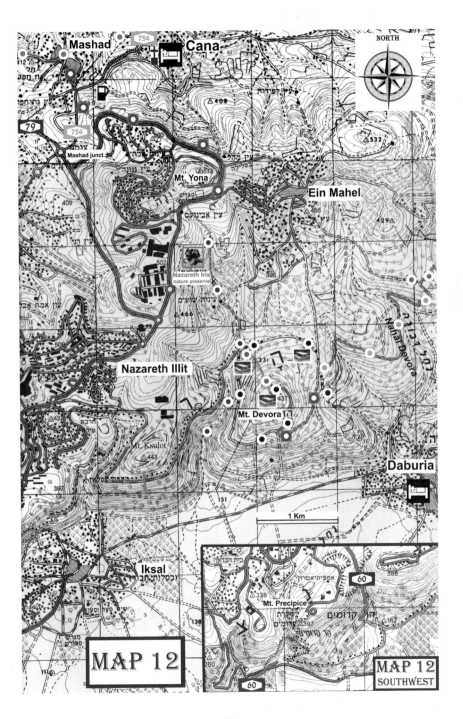

Statue of the Visitation – Ein Kerem, Jerusalem
The rock behind which Elizabeth and Zacharia hid

MAP 13

SURVEY OF ISRAEL

JERUSALEM

LEGEND

Built-up area, Public building ....

Public park or Woodland.........................

Synagogue ⚋   Church ⚊   Mosque ⚋

Main road, divided ....

Road, Tunnel, Bridge ....

Unpaved road, Fuel station...........

Promenade or Pedestrian Mall ......

Railway ....

Motorway, Highway ....

Main street ....

Other street...........................

Interurban road numbers:

Motorway ①   Highway ⑥⓪

Regional road ④④⑥   Local road ③⑨⑧⑤

Jerusalem trail

Scale

0	100	200	300	400	500	600	700	800	900	1000

Metres   Metres

89

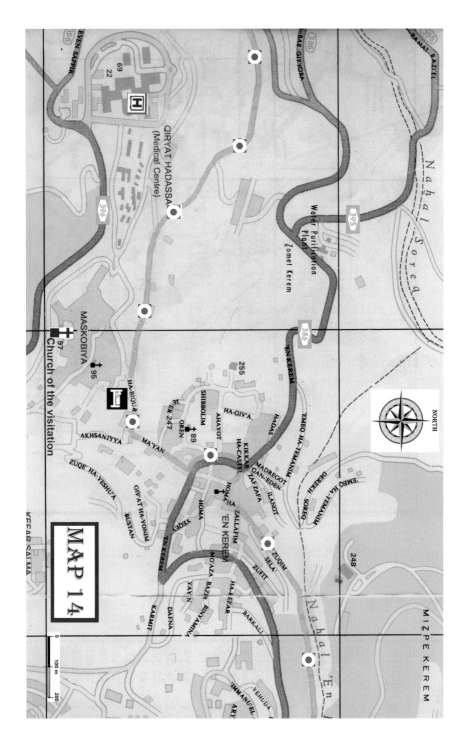

MAP 14

EVEN SAPPIR
396
69
22
H
QIRYAT HADASSA
(Medical Centre)
396
BAR GIYYORA
386
Water Purification Plant
395
Zomet Kerem
Nahal Soreq
RAMAT RAZIEL
395
386
NORTH
248
MISPE KEREM
Nahal 'En
MASKOBIYA
97
Church of the visitation
95
HA-BIQU'A
255
SHIBBOLIM
HA-GIV'A
EN KEREM
HADAS
'EMEQ HA-TEMANIM
247
OREN
89
AHAYOT
KIKKAR GAN-'EDEN
MADREGOT
DEREKH SOREQ
'EMEQ HA-TEMANIM
AKHSANIYYA
MA'YAN
HA-CASTEL
ZAF-ZAFA
ILANOT
ZUQE' HA-YESHU'A
GIV'AT HA-YONIM
HOMA HA
ZALLAFIM
'EN KEREM
ZUQIM
BUSTAN
'EN KEREM
HOMA
YEDID
SELA'
ZUFIT
MO'AZA
HA-EFAR
BARKALI
DAFNA
KARMIT
BAZIR
BINYAMINA
YAYN
IMMANU'EL
ARY
YEHUDA
KEFAR SALMA

0
100 m
200

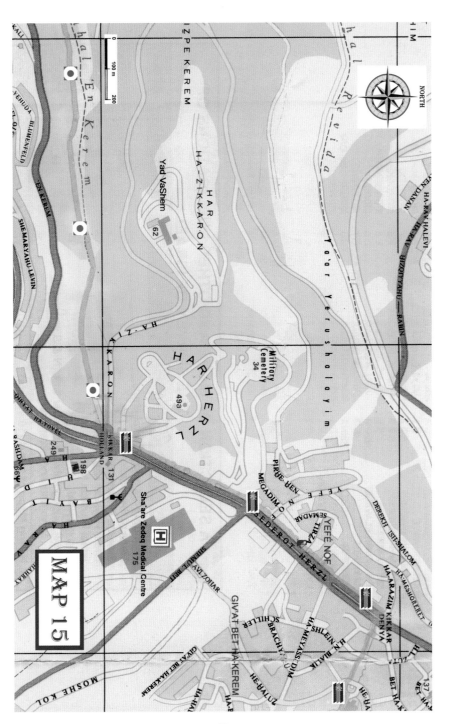

MAP 15

NORTH

0 100 m 200

Yad VaShem
62

HAR
HA-ZIKKARON

IZPE KEREM

'En Kerem

hal 'En Kerem

SHE MARYAHU LEVIN

'EN KEREM

BLUMENFELD

YEHUDA

KALI

Ya'ar Yerushalayim

hal Revida

HA-RAV HALEVI

HA-RAV HERZL

HIZQIYAHU—RABIN

BEN DANAN

HA-ZIK—KARON

HAR HERZL

Military
Cemetery
34

49a

Sha'are Zedeq Medical Centre
175

KIKKAR 131

HOLLAND

249

198

199

BAYIT

HA

QIRYAT HA-YOVEL

ASHDAM

MEGADIM

NER ARIE

SEDEROT HERZL

YEFE NOF

SEMADAR

TIRZA

PIRHE

DEREKH ISTE-SHALOM

HA-MESHORERET

HA-ARAZIM KIKKAR
DENYA

HA-AVI ZOHAR

SHMUEL BEIT

GIVAT BET HA-KEREM

BRACHYA

SCHILLER

H. N. BIALIK

HA-MESAB'IM

HA-SHLEIN-DIN

BET HA-

137

MOSHE KOL

GIVAT BET HA-KEREM

HE-HALUZ

HE-HA

91

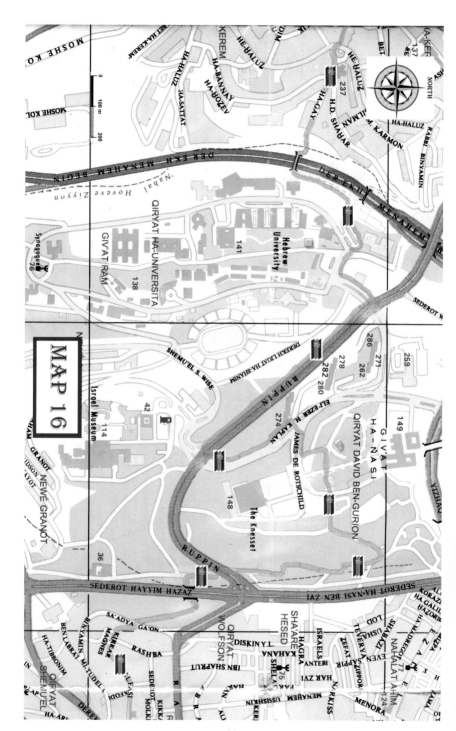

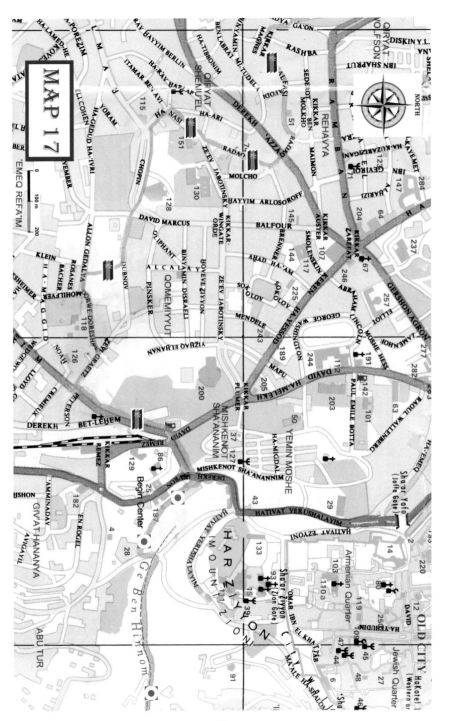

MAP 17

Room of the Last Supper

Russian Orthodox Church of Mary Magdalene on Mt. of Olives (left)
Hagia Maria Sion Abbey - Dormition of the Virgin Mary on Mt. Zion (right)

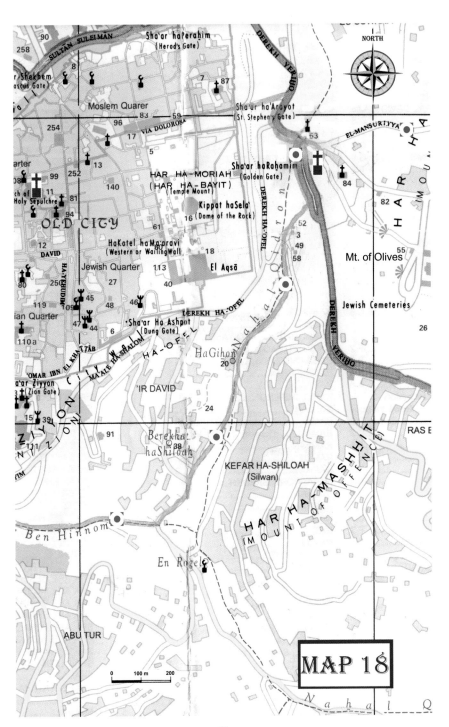

MAP 18

Dome of the Rock – View from Mt. of Olives

The Holy Sepulchre, Ninth Station (left)
The Tomb of Christ, Fourteenth Station (right)